Unveiled Faces

Fasting & Praying Manual

Written By:

By Dr. Sheka Mansaray

{F.E.I.M}

Faith Embassy International Ministries

(Revelation Church)

Revelation Publishing
Kingdom Revelation fit to print

Table of Contents

Dedication & Acknowledgements

I acknowledge the almighty God for His amazing and uncommon blessing, grace, favor, wisdom, vision, insight and faith in my life. I sincerely acknowledge my beautiful wife Dr. Nanah Mansaray for standing beside me throughout the writing of this book. You have been my inspiration and motivation for continuing to improve my knowledge and to know when to take a break and to move forward one step at a time.

To my sons and daughters in the Lord, the ministers, who had been supportive and sharing my happiness when starting this book and following with encouragement and to see the work completed, I say to you all thank you.

To all "Faith Embassy International Ministries – Revelation Church-" Branches around the world, thank you family for all of your support and prayer, And to my children, daughter, Faith Mansaray; and Son, Sheka Jeremiah Mansaray Jr. and son, Joseph Ezekiel Mansaray.

He will see His face

And we all, who with unveiled faces contemplate[a] the Lord's glory, are being transformed into his image with ever-increasing glory, which comes from the Lord, who is the Spirit. 2 Corinthians 3:18

let their flesh be renewed like a child's; let them be restored as in the days of their youth'--Job 33:25

He will pray to God and find favor; he will see His face and shout for joy, and God will restore the righteousness of that man. Job 33:26

Unveiled faces

O Lord, our God Unveil the faces of our souls
The faces withdrawn
The faces of predators
These faces are bitten
by dispositions downcast
by unearthly cry,

The faces withdrawn
O Lord, our God Unveil the faces of our souls
The spiritual prophetic face's
These faces tolerate testimony tale of predators
While we lay yet awake,
They show their lineage from their Master who masked them

The faces withdrawn
The sacred faces
father Do you suppose we could content their own finale?
These faces await the testimony
To withdraw the smiles of the predators faces
Those then are not mankind, or superiors yet they gather
great being round the globe
O Lord, our God Unveil the faces of our souls.
By Dr. Sheka Mansaray

How to Begin Your Fast

How to Begin Your Fast How you begin and conduct your fast will largely determine your success. By following these seven basic steps to fasting, you will make your time with the Lord more meaningful and spiritually rewarding.

STEP 1: Set Your Objective Why are you fasting? Is it for spiritual renewal, for guidance, for healing, for the resolution of problems, for special grace to handle a difficult situation? Ask the Holy Spirit to clarify His leading and objectives for your prayer fast. This will enable you to pray more specifically and strategically. Through fasting and prayer we humble ourselves before God so the Holy Spirit will stir our souls, awaken our churches, and heal our land according to 2 Chronicles 7:14. Make this a priority in your fasting.

STEP 2: Make Your Commitment Pray about the kind of fast you should undertake. Jesus implied that all of His followers should fast (Matthew 6:16-18; 9:14,15) For Him it was a matter of when believers would fast, not if they would do it. Before you fast, decide the following up front:

• How long you will fast - one meal, one day, a week, several weeks, forty days (Beginners should start slowly, building up to longer fasts.)

• The type of fast God wants you to undertake (such as water only, or water and juices; what kinds of juices you will drink and how often)

• What physical or social activities you will restrict

• How much time each day you will devote to prayer and God's Word Making these commitments ahead of time will help you sustain your fast when physical temptations and life's pressures tempt you to abandon it.

STEP 3: Prepare Yourself Spiritually The very foundation of fasting and prayer is repentance. Unconfessed sin will hinder your prayers. Here are several things you can do to prepare your heart:

• Ask God to help you make a comprehensive list of your sins.

• Confess every sin that the Holy Spirit calls to your remembrance and accept God's forgiveness (1 John 1:9).

• Seek forgiveness from all whom you have offended, and forgive all who have hurt you (Mark 11:25; Luke 11:4; 17:3,4).

• Make restitution as the Holy Spirit leads you.

Ask God to fill you with His Holy Spirit according to His command in Ephesians 5:18 and His promise in 1 John 5:14,15.

• Surrender your life fully to Jesus Christ as your Lord and Master; refuse to obey your worldly nature (Romans 12:1,2).

• Meditate on the attributes of God, His love, sovereignty, power, wisdom, faithfulness, grace, compassion, and others (Psalm 48:9,10; 103:1-8, 11-13).

• Begin your time of fasting and prayer with an expectant heart (Hebrews 11:6).

• Do not underestimate spiritual opposition. Satan sometimes intensifies the natural battle between body and spirit (Galatians 5:16,17).

STEP 4: Prepare Yourself Physically Fasting requires reasonable precautions. Consult your physician first, especially if you take prescription medication or have a chronic ailment. Some persons should never fast without professional supervision. Physical preparation makes the drastic change in your eating routine a little easier so that you can turn your full attention to the Lord in prayer.

• Do not rush into your fast.

• Prepare your body. Eat smaller meals before starting a fast. Avoid high-fat and sugary foods.

• Eat raw fruit and vegetables for two days before starting a fast. While You Fast Your time of fasting and prayer has come. You are abstaining from all solid foods and have begun to seek the Lord. Here are some helpful suggestions to consider:

• Avoid drugs, even natural herbal drugs and homeopathic remedies. Medication should be withdrawn only with your physician's supervision.

• Limit your activity.

• Exercise only moderately. Walk one to three miles each day if convenient and comfortable.

• Rest as much as your schedule will permit.

• Prepare yourself for temporary mental discomforts, such as impatience, crankiness, and anxiety.

• Expect some physical discomforts, especially on the second -day. You may have fleeting hunger pains, dizziness, or the "blahs." Withdrawal from caffeine and sugar may cause headaches. Physical annoyances may also include weakness, tiredness, or sleeplessness.

The first two or three days are usually the hardest. As you continue to fast, you will likely experience a sense of well-being both physically and spiritually. However, should you feel hunger pains, increase your liquid intake.

STEP 5: Put Yourself on a Schedule For maximum spiritual benefit, set aside ample time to be alone with the Lord. Listen for His leading. The more time you spend with Him, the more meaningful your fast will be. Morning,

• Begin your day in praise and worship.

Read and meditate on God's Word, preferably on your knees.

• Invite the Holy Spirit to work in you to will and to do His good pleasure according to Philippians 2:13.

• Invite God to use you. Ask Him to show you how to influence your world, your family, your church, your community, your country, and beyond.

• Pray for His vision for your life and empowerment to do His will. Noon

• Return to prayer and God's Word.

• Take a short prayer walk.

• Spend time in intercessory prayer for your community's and nation's leaders, for the world's unreached millions, for your family or special needs. Evening

• Get alone for an unhurried time of "seeking His face."

• If others are fasting with you, meet together for prayer.

• Avoid television or any other distraction that may dampen your spiritual focus. When possible, begin and end each day on your knees with your spouse for a brief time of praise and thanksgiving to God. Longer periods of time with our Lord in prayer and study of His Word are often better spent alone. A dietary routine is vital as well – I suggests a daily schedule and list of juices you may find useful and satisfying. Modify this schedule and the drinks you take to suit your circumstances and tastes. 5 a.m. - 8 a.m.

• Fruit juices, preferably freshly squeezed or blended and diluted in 50 percent distilled water if the fruit is acid. Apple, pear, grapefruit, papaya, watermelon, or other fruit juices are generally preferred. If you cannot do your own juicing, buy juices without sugar or additives. 10:30 a.m. - noon

• Fresh vegetable juice made from lettuce, celery, and carrots in three equal parts. 2:30 p.m. - 4 p.m.

• Herb tea with a drop of honey. Avoid black tea or any tea with caffeine. 6 p.m. - 8:30 p.m.

• Broth made from boiling potatoes, celery, and carrots with no salt. After boiling about half an hour, pour the water into a container and drink it. Tips on Juice Fasting

• Drinking fruit juice will decrease your hunger pains and give you some natural sugar energy. The taste and lift will motivate and strengthen you to continue.

• The best juices are made from fresh watermelon, lemons, grapes, apples, cabbage, beets, carrots, celery, or leafy green vegetables. In cold weather, you may enjoy a warm vegetable broth.

• Mix acidic juices (orange and tomato) with water for your stomach's sake.

• Avoid caffeinated drinks. And avoid chewing gum or mints, even if your breath is bad. They stimulate digestive action in your stomach. Breaking Your Fast When your designated time for fasting is finished, you will begin to eat again. But how you break your fast is extremely important for your physical and spiritual well-being.

STEP 6: End Your Fast Gradually Begin eating gradually. Do not eat solid foods immediately after your fast. Suddenly reintroducing solid food to your stomach and digestive tract will likely have negative, even dangerous, consequences. Try several smaller meals or snacks each day. If you end your fast gradually, the beneficial physical and spiritual effects will result in continued good health.

Here are some suggestions to help you end your fast properly:

• Break an extended water fast with fruit such as watermelon.

• While continuing to drink fruit or vegetable juices, add the following: First day: Add a raw salad. Second day: Add baked or boiled potato, no butter or seasoning. Third day: Add a steamed vegetable. Thereafter: Begin to reintroduce your normal diet.

• Gradually return to regular eating with several small snacks during the first few days. Start with a little soup and fresh fruit such as watermelon and cantaloupe. to a few tablespoons of solid foods such as raw fruits and vegetables or a raw salad and baked potato.

STEP 7: Expect Results If you sincerely humble yourself before the Lord, repent, pray, and seek God's face; if you consistently meditate on His Word, you will experience a heightened awareness of His presence (John 14:21). The Lord will give you fresh, new spiritual insights. Your confidence and faith in God will be strengthened. You will feel mentally, spiritually, and physically refreshed. You will see answers to your prayers. A single fast, however, is not a spiritual cure-all. Just as we need fresh infillings of the Holy Spirit daily, we also need new times of fasting before God. A 24-hour fast each week has been greatly rewarding to many Christians. It takes time to build your spiritual fasting muscles. If you fail to make it through your first fast, do not be discouraged. You may have tried to fast too long the first time out, or your may need to strengthen your understanding and resolve. As soon as possible, undertake another fast until you do succeed. God will honor you for your faithfulness. I encourage you to join me in fasting and prayer again and again until we truly experience revival in our homes, our churches, our beloved nation, and throughout the world. How to Experience and Maintain Personal Revival

1. Ask the Holy Spirit to reveal any unconfessed sin in your life.

2. Seek forgiveness from all whom you have offended, and forgive all who have hurt you. Make restitution where God leads.

3. Examine your motives in every word and deed. Ask the Lord to search and cleanse your heart daily.

4. Ask the Holy Spirit to guard your walk against complacency and mediocrity.

5. Praise and give thanks to God continually in all ways on all days, regardless of your circumstances.

6. Refuse to obey your carnal (worldly) nature (Galatians 5:16,17).

7. Surrender your life to Jesus Christ as your Savior and Lord. Develop utter dependence on Him with total submission and humility.

8. Study the attributes of God.

9. Hunger and thirst after righteousness (Matthew 5:6).

10. Love God with all of your heart, soul, and mind (Matthew 22:37).

11. Appropriate the continual fullness and control of the Holy Spirit by faith on the basis of God's command (Ephesians 5:18) and promise (1 John 5:14,15).

12. Read, study, meditate on, and memorize God's holy, inspired, inerrant Word daily (Colossians 3:16). 13. Pray without ceasing (1 Thessalonians 5:17).

14. Fast and pray one 24-hour period each week. Prayerfully consider becoming one of the two million Christians who will fast for forty days before the start/end of the year.

15. Seek to share Christ daily as a way of life.

16. Determine to live a holy, godly life of obedience and faith.

17. Start or join a home or church Bible study group that emphasizes revival and a holy life.

6 Vital Questions About Prayer

Q: What Is Prayer? Simply put, prayer is communicating with God. Real prayer is expressing our devotion to our heavenly Father, inviting Him to talk to us as we talk to Him.

Q: Who Can Pray? Anyone can pray, but only those who walk in faith and obedience to Christ can expect to receive answers to their prayers.

Contact with God begins when we receive Jesus into our lives as Savior and Lord (John 14:6). Praying with a clean heart is also vital to successful prayer. We cannot expect God to answer our prayers if there is any unconfessed sin in our life or if we are harboring an unforgiving spirit (Psalm 66:18; Mark 11:25). For God to answer our prayers, we must have a believing heart and ask according to His will (Matthew 9:29; 21:22; 1 John 5:14,15).

Q: Why Are We to Pray? God's Word commands us to pray (Luke 18:1; Acts 6:4; Mark 14:38; Philippians 4:6; Colossians 4:2; 1 Timothy 2:1,2). We pray to have fellowship with God, receive spiritual nurture and strength to live a victorious life, and maintain boldness for a vital witness for Christ. Prayer releases God's great power to change the course of nature, people, and nations.

Q: To Whom Do We Pray? We pray to the Father in the name of the Lord Jesus Christ through the ministry of the Holy Spirit. when we pray to the Father, our prayers are accepted by Jesus Christ and interpreted to God the Father by the Holy Spirit (Romans 8:26, 27,34).

Q: When Should We Pray? God's Word commands us to "Pray continually" (1 Thessalonians 5:17). We can be in prayer throughout the day, expressing and demonstrating our devotion to God as we go about our daily tasks. It is not always necessary to be on our knees, or even in a quiet room to pray. God wants us to be in touch with Him constantly wherever we are. We can pray in the car, while washing the dishes, or while walking down the street.

Q: What Should We Include in Our Prayers? Although prayer cannot be reduced to a formula, certain basic elements should be included in our communication with God: Adoration, Confession, Thanksgiving, Supplication (ACTS). A-Adoration To adore God is to worship and praise Him, to honor and exalt Him in our heart and mind and with our lips.

Introduction

This book is a Manual written for Faith Embassy International Ministries (F.E.l.M) (Revelation Church). This fasting is for our Annual 21 Days Fasting & Praying every January which is titled (Unveiled the Faces OF Prayer)

I have a question for you... I wonder whether if you have ever fasted?

I wonder whether it has even occurred to us that we should consider the question of fasting? The fact is, is it not, that this whole subject seems to have dropped right out of our lives and right out of our whole Christian thinking –It was not Christ's intention to reject or despise fasting... it was His intention to restore proper fasting.

To fast and pray is something strange to many Christians today. But it is not strange to the Old or the New Testament. It was not something strange in the early Christian Church and it was also not something strange in the time of the Reformation and in the centuries thereafter. Moses, Elijah, Ezekiel and Daniel fasted and prayed. Jesus fasted for 40 days. Paul and the early Christians fasted. In the early Christian Church they fasted on Wednesdays and Fridays.

who satisfies your desires with good things so that your youth is renewed like the eagle's. Psalm 103:5

Satisfy us in the morning with Your loving devotion, that we may sing for joy and be glad all our days. Psalm 90:14

For He satisfies the thirsty and fills the hungry with good things. Psalm 107:9

You open Your hand and satisfy the desire of every living thing. Psalm 145:16

A righteous man eats to his heart's content, but the stomach of the wicked is empty. Proverbs 13:25

But those who wait upon the LORD will renew their strength; they will mount up with wings like eagles; they will run and not grow weary; they will walk and not faint. Isaiah 40:31

"And we, who with unveiled faces all reflect the Lord's glory, are being transformed into his likeness with ever-increasing glory, which comes from the Lord, who is the Spirit" (NIV). 2 Corinthians 3:18

Paul is taking the readers back to Moses. Moses would walk up to this mountain called Mount Sinai. There he would meet with God face-to-face. It was the place where God gave Moses the Ten Commandments. Each time Moses went to meet with God on this mountain, he came back glowing.

He had an encounter with God on Mount Sinai, and this encounter was so remarkable that Moses was transformed. His appearance was altered. He shone. He looked different. The first time he came down from the mountain, people were even afraid. The change was that significant.

Moses would wear a veil over his face when he came down from the mountain. He wore a veil to cover the fading glory (2 Cor. 3:13). Once Moses left the presence of God, the glory would fade. With each step away from the mountain, the glory would decrease.

Moses had a veiled face. We have unveiled faces.

We do not have to wear a veil because the glory is not diminishing. In fact the opposite is true. The glory is ever increasing. It is so because we never leave the presence of God. We never come back down the mountain.

The mountain is in us.

His Spirit lives within us. We have a relationship with God that even Moses did not have. We are in the new covenant that brings righteousness, not the old covenant that brings death (2 Cor. 3:9). Moses had to go to the mountain to behold the glory of God. We don't. We have a greater level of intimacy.

Just as God transformed Moses, He transforms us when we place ourselves in His presence. The word for transform is in the passive voice and present tense. The passive voice indicates that we do not transform ourselves. God is the one who does the transforming.

The present tense indicates that this transforming is currently taking place. Right now. As you read this. Transformation is not only a past event. God is also about right now.

The word from transformation is metamorphosis. It means to change the essential nature of something. It is a real change, not just a change on the outside. The core of something is changed. The word is used to describe the process a caterpillar goes through to become a butterfly. The nasty, wormy, creepy, crawly insect becomes a beautiful butterfly. The process is metamorphosis.

God desires to bring His people through this morphing process. He seeks to transform the people in your church into His image. And He wants to do so with ever-increasing glory. Meaning He wants the people you serve to be more like Him tomorrow than they are today.

Jonathan Edwards who was God's instrument in the revival in New England, fasted and prayed. John Wesley fasted twice a week. Charles Finney one of the greatest spiritual leaders in history was a man who fasted and prayed. D L Moody was not unfamiliar with fasting and praying.

Principles

1. There is more to fasting than just abstaining from food —fasting is about our relationship with Christ, it is a spiritual exercise with a focus, a Christ –centered purpose seeking spiritual results that honor and glorify Christ (see Isaiah 58:1ff; Matt 6:16-18; Ezra 9:1-10)

2. Fasting is a help to our life of prayer (John 15; 1 Thess 5:17; Neh 1:8-10)

3. Fasting is expected and taught to be a practiced discipline of the faith (Matt 6:16-18; 9:14-15)

4. Fasting was associated with grief and mourning (1 Sam 1:7-8; 31:13)

5. Fasting was associated with seeking God's renewed presence and sustaining strength and salvation from enemies, danger and temptation (Ex 34:28; Matt 4:1-11; Lk 4:2; 2 Chron 20:3-4; Esther 4:16;)

6. Fasting goes along with knowing and doing God's will (Judges 20; Acts 14:23)

7. Fasting is related to power and fruit through ministry (1 Kings 13:1-22; Isa 58:1-12; Acts 13:1-4; Matt 4:2ff)

8. Fasting is linked with worship and adoration of the Father (Luke 2:37; Zechariah 7:5)

Practices

1. The Bible distinguishes between several kinds of fasts: normal (all food but not water, Matt 4:2), partial (dietary limitation, Dan 1:12), absolute, (no food or liquids, Ezra 10:6), supernatural (Deut. 9:9)

2. In Scripture fasts were private (Matt 6:16-18), congregational (Joel 2:15-16; Acts 13:1-4), regular and occasional fasts (Lev 16:29-31; Matt 9:15)

3. Biblical fasts lasted— (see Judges 20:26; Acts 9:9; 1 Sam 31:13; Dan 10:3-13) Practical Tips Bill Bright's 7 Basic Steps to Successful Fasting and Prayer—

a. Set your Objectives—search motives, set goals, prayer points, humble yourself before God (2 Chron 7:14)

b. Ask the Spirit to show you the kind of fast—length, focus, kind, limitations on activity, God's Word

c. Prepare Spiritually—list sins, confess, repent, seek forgiveness, make restitution, filled with the Spirit, surrender, meditate on God and His word, pray with expectation, be prepared for Spiritual opposition

d. Prepare Physically--gradually move into a long fast, eat smaller meals avoid high fat, sugar, eat raw veggies and fruits before fast. When Fasting—avoid drugs if possible— even natural herbal remedies, limit activity, exercise moderately, walk for exercise, rest, expect headaches, impatience, physical discomforts, keep liquids flowing— juices, herbal teas, broth,

e. Put yourself on a schedule—worship, read the word, pray, surrender to God's purposes and activity, pray for vision, take walks, pray during meals, seek His heart in unceasing prayer, avoid TV, meet with others to pray, pray with spouse and family

f. End Your Fast Gradually—replace water with fruit juice, broths, soups, utilize small snacks, etc.

g. Expect Results—a fast is not a spiritual cure all—keep relationship centered!

What does it mean to fast and pray?

1. To fast means to put God first. There are times when we have to eat and drink and sleep and enjoy the blessings of a homely life. But there are also times when we have to turn our backs on it and seek God's face in times of fasting and praying. Fasting is an attitude of the heart in which we interrupt our normal life to pray for a specific matter or cause.
2. Fasting also means perseverance in prayer. It means to be earnest with God; to pray until you have found the answer - be it yes or no or wait a while.
3. Fasting is an effective way to remove obstacles and burdens to pray purposefully and with your attention.
4. Fasting can also be a sign of sadness or mourning but it also contains an element of firmness.
5. In the Old Testament they often fasted as a sign of humiliation (Lev.23:27) In its essence fasting means that we tear our hearts before God, confess our sins and turn to the Lord anew (Joel 2:12-13). 2
6. The Lord also intended fasting to sometimes have an element of happiness and joy (Zech.8:19).
7. In Isaiah 58:6-7 we find the attitude we should have whilst fasting and praying, which results in the blessings promised in Isaiah 58:8-14. The Lord Jesus set only one

condition to fasting and that is sincerity. He does not forbid it anywhere and neither does He say that it is unnecessary to fast and pray. In Matthew 6:16-18 Jesus gives certain prescriptions for fasting. Fasting and praying is a more intense form of praying. It could be that you have been praying for a certain matter for years without an answer. There is but one alternative: fast and pray. Fasting and praying always lead to more personal sanctification and God listens to a prayer from a pure heart. Fasting and praying also stresses your seriousness about a matter before God. Some situations demand that we as intercessors should fast and pray. There is sufficient evidence of what effect fasting and prayer has had in the course of the history of many countries and many other situations.

8. B. What can we gain through fasting and praying?
9. Help in times of need (Josh.7:6; Judges 20:26; Ezra 8:21-23) In the past fasting brought deliverance in times of crisis and for specific situations.
10. To find out what is wrong. Sometimes we have to fast and pray like Joshua and the elder after they had suffered defeat at Ai to find out what went wrong.
11. It can help to bring us into a position of victory over sin.

12. We can obtain heavenly wisdom and revelation through fasting and prayer (Jer.33:3; Dan.9:2-3; 9:21-22; 10:2-3)
13. Others often experience a blessing when we fast and pray for them (e.g. unsaved people or people in some or other crisis)
14. In history revival was often given in answer to fasting and prayer.
15. We find in Esther 4 that a nation was saved because of fasting and prayer.
16. God saved Nineveh because the inhabitants fasted, prayed and repented (Jonah 2 and 3)
17. Look at the blessings promised in Isaiah 58:8-14 that follow true fasting and prayer.
18. Fasting keeps us humble (Ps.69:10)
19. Fasting chastises the body and helps us to gain control over our bodies (1 Cor.9:27; 1 Cor.6:13-20)
20. C. Different forms of fasting.
21. An ordinary fast: when you take no solids for a certain period and drink only water.
22. A complete fast: to take no water or any other form of food for a certain period.
23. A partial fast: to omit certain foods for a certain period (e.g. sweets) and/or to eat and drink less. During a partial fast someone might decide to eat bread and drink water only.

The don'ts of fasting

• Don't fast to earn God's blessings

- Don't fast as a substitute to obedience

- Don't fast to impress others

- Don't allow fasting to be only external

- Don't allow fasting to become a new law in your life. Many people are afraid to fast but as long as there are no medical reasons why you should not fast, there is no danger. It is even good for your body. The second and third days are normally slightly difficult because of the changes the body has to make and due to the toxic substances your body secretes but things do become better after that. If you have never fasted before it would not be wise to fast and pray for more than 36 hours. You can always extend the period as you become more familiar with fasting and praying. Don't try to prove something to others by fasting or try to set a record. Fasting is a very intimate matter between you and the Lord. Allow the Holy Spirit to lead you as to how long you should fast and pray. Somebody on a normal fast can fast for quite some time (up to 21 days) without risk. In recent times many thousand of people have fasted for 40 days. But the latter should only be done on commission of the Lord.

E. Practical guidelines for fasting and prayer.

- If you have never fasted before you should not fast for more than 24-36 hours initially.
- Stop taking fluids containing caffeine the previous day. The withdrawal of caffeine normally causes headaches.

- People used to taking a lot of sugar find fasting very difficult. Keep up your fast though and when you have completed it you should try using less sugar.
- Don't fast without fluids for longer than three days. o When you break your fast start by eating something light. Don't eat a large plate of food. Get back to normal slowly. It is normally a good time to break the habit of overeating, if you have a problem with it.

• The body excretes an excessive amount of toxic waste during the first three days. Shower or bath regularly and brush your teeth more than usual because you may have foul smelling breath, especially during the first three days.

• Try to find as much time for prayer as possible. Normally you do not need to stop your normal activities. You can fast even though you work a full day. You can even indulge in light forms of sport and exercise. You can for instance use the times that you would be eating for prayer and put as much time as possible aside for fellowship with the Lord.

• When you fast and pray it is best to break with your normal routine and go aside to pray in a quiet spot.

• The normal items you would need during fasting and prayer are a Bible, pen, note book, and perhaps a spiritual book that you are reading at that point in time. Make notes about that which the Lord lays upon your heart. Write new thoughts down. Don't rely on your memory, write them down.

• Don't fast while working with a demon possessed or bound person. Fast and pray before the time. When you are working with such a case you will need physical strength.

• It is a good idea to have other believers fast and pray with you. You can encourage each other and it is encouraging to know that there are others praying for the same matter.

• If there are medical reasons why you cannot fast don't feel guilty about it and do not be wilful. Diabetics and people suffering from a heart disorder should rather not fast. Consult your doctor if you have any doubt about it.

• If you have fasted for guidance from the Lord and experience that you have received guidance do not be hasty. Wait until the fast is over, especially if you are fasting for a long period. It will give you a better perspective on the matter.

• Fasting is a matter between you and the Lord, therefore don't copy others.

• Drink plenty of water while you fast.

• When you have fasted for more than three days it is important to remember to:

> • start eating small portions of food
> • eat slowly o chew your food well

o stop eating if you experience discomfort o wait for the feeling of discomfort to disappear before eating again o don't do too much too soon.

F. When should we fast?

• We should fast when the Holy Spirit lays it on our hearts (Luke 4:1-2)

• When an individual has a particular need, for instance: o if someone asks the Lord's Will in a particular matter

- for your own preparation for a certain task;
- in times of heavy attacks or temptations of the evil one o when the individual feels that he should make more time for the Lord to replenish his spiritual strength
  - when we are confronted with specific strongholds of the evil one.

G. Hot to go aside for a day. Many people want to go aside and be alone with God for a day. The question is: What do I do all day? The following are a few ideas on how to schedule such a day. You can see if it will work for you for yourself. Remember these are only ideas to stimulate you. The important thing is to fill the day as it suits you.

• You can start by going aside for only a morning or an afternoon or an evening. If you can fill in half a day you can extend the period.

• Get a note book, a Bible, a pen and if you want to a good spiritual book. Pick a quiet place without telephones where you can be undisturbed. Decide for how long you want to be busy and try to stick to it.

• Start your time with the Lord with exaltation, worship and just being quiet in the presence of the Lord.

• If your mind starts wandering and you think of everything you have to do, write it down on a sheet of paper. In doing so you ensure that you will not forget and can pay attention to it later.

• Select a book from the Bible and start reading it from the beginning. For example you can start reading Psalm 1, or you can take a book like Ephesians. Don't be in a hurry. Take it verse by verse; ask the Lord what He wants to teach you from that verse, reflect on the verse, pray about it. When you have finished with that verse, carry on and do the same with the next one. Write down the important things that the Lord is saying to you in your note book.

• After 30-60 minutes of Bible study you can go into direct prayer. Take time for confession and take a hard look at your own relationship with the Lord. After this you can pray for your personal needs or for specific matters. This can be followed by intercession. It is very important not to be in a hurry. The emphasis should be on fellowship with the Lord.

• You have perhaps set this time aside to pray for certain matters specifically or to seek the Lord's guidance. In that case make time to pray specifically for that.

• Vary your time with Bible study and prayer. Also take time to read a few chapters of a spiritual book.

• You may even sleep for a while if you feel like it. At the end of the day you will be revived and ready to get to work again. If possible it is also a good idea to listen to some Christian music from time to time.

• When a whole group of people are withdrawing (going aside) for a day at the same time, you can follow the above guidelines and get together every two or three hours and share what you have experienced and also pray together.

I believe the power of fasting as it relates to prayer is the spiritual atomic bomb that our Lord has given us to destroy the strongholds of evil and usher in a great revival and spiritual harvest around the world. Increasingly I have been gripped with a growing sense of urgency to call upon God to send revival to our beloved countries. In the spring and summer of 2011, I had a growing conviction that God wanted me to fast and pray for forty days for revival in America and around the world and for the fulfillment of the Great Commission in obedience to our Lord's command. At first I questioned, "Is this truly God's call for me?" Forty days was a long time to go without solid food. But with each passing day, His call grew stronger and more clear.

Finally, I was convinced. God was calling me to fast, and He would not make such a call without a specific reason or purpose. With this conviction, I entered my fast with excitement and expectancy mounting in my heart, praying, "Lord, what do you want me to do?"

I believe such a long fast was a sovereign call of God because of the magnitude of the sins of the Church. The Lord impressed that upon my heart, as well as the urgent need to help accelerate the fulfillment of the Great Commission in this generation. As I began my fast, I was not sure I could continue for forty days. But my confidence was in the Lord to help me. Each day His presence encouraged me to continue. The longer I fasted, the more I sensed the presence of the Lord. The Holy Spirit refreshed my soul and spirit, and I experienced the joy of the Lord as seldom before. Biblical truths leaped at me from the pages of God's Word. My faith soared as I humbled myself and cried out to God and rejoiced in His presence.

This proved to be the most important forty days of my life. As I waited upon the Lord, the Holy Spirit gave me the assurance that America and much of the world will, before the end of the year, experience a great spiritual awakening. This divine visit from heaven will kindle the greatest spiritual harvest in the history of the Church. But before God comes in revival power, the Holy Spirit will call millions of God's people to repent, fast, and pray in the spirit of 2 Chronicles 7:14: If my people, who are called by my name, will humble themselves and pray and seek my face and turn from their wicked ways, then I will hear from heaven and will forgive their sin and will heal their land.

The scope of this revival depends on how believers in America and the rest of the world respond to this call. I have spent fifty years studying God's Word and listening to His voice, and His message could not have been clearer, will help make your time with the Lord more spiritually rewarding. I encourage you to keep it with you during your fast and refer to it often because it gives easy-to-follow suggestions on how to begin your fast, what to do while you fast, and how to end your fast properly. During my forty-day fast, God impressed me to pray that two million Christians in the world will fast for forty days by the end of the year , and pray for national and worldwide revival and for the fulfillment of the Great Commission. I urge you to prayerfully consider this challenge. Before you fast, I encourage you to read my book, The Coming Revival: the World/ nations Call to Fast, Pray, and "Seek God's Face." It will help equip you for the coming spiritual awakening.

Spiritual Awakening for fasting

WHILE FASTING Jesus answered, "It is written: 'Man shall not live on bread alone, but on every word that comes from the mouth of God.'" MATTHEW 4:4 Focus—

Set aside time to work through the devotionals. Be ready to respond to God's Word and the leading of the Holy Spirit. Pray—Join at least one prayer meeting in your local church. Intercede for your family, church, pastors, nation, campuses, and missions throughout the week. Replenish—During mealtime, read the Bible and pray instead. Drink plenty of water and rest as much as you can. Be ready for temporary bouts of physical weakness and mental annoyances like impatience and irritability.

"Then you shall call, and the Lord will answer; you shall cry, and he will say, 'Here I am.'" ISAIAH 58:9 (ESV) Eat —Reintroduce solid food gradually. Your body will need time to adjust to a normal diet. Start with fruits, juices, and salad, then add more vegetables. Eat small portions throughout the day. Pray—Don't give up! Trust God's faithfulness and timing. Carry your newfound passion for God throughout the year. Be in faith for God to answer your prayers.

ANSWERED PRAYERS

List highlights, answered prayers, and lessons learned in the year before. Thank God for His faithfulness, provision, and grace this year! A Practical Guide to Prayer and Fasting I am believing God for . . .

PERSONAL FAITH GOALS Spiritual Revival

- Physical Healing
- Prosperity and Abundance
- Rich Generosity
- MY FAMILY Restoration of Relationships
- Household Salvation
- MY SCHOOL/CAREER Excellence
- Promotion
- MY MINISTRY Small Group Growth
- Salvation of Colleagues, Classmates, Bosses, Employees

PRAYERS FOR THE BODY OF CHRIST

PRAYERS FOR THE BODY OF CHRIST

SCRIPTURES Phil. 2 v9 – 11; Eph. 6 v 10 – 18; Mathew 18 v 18 – 20

ENCOURAGEMENT

The body of Christ needs prayer, and we as part of the Church need to arise and cry unto God for her so that the Church will not cease to be relevant in this generation. We have to pray that God will empower the Church Universally in order to triumphantly march over the kingdom of darkness and establish righteousness in every nations of the world. PRAYERS Song: The Church is marching on /2ce The gate of hell shall not prevail The Church is marching on.

1. O Lord, protect your interest in all your Churches all over the world and let no corruption enter the Church in Jesus name.

2. Let every host of darkness that is assigned against the body of Christ for calamity, be scattered and rendered powerless in Jesus name.

3. Let every activity of hell be destroyed over the body of Christ in Jesus name.

4. Let unity, love, righteousness, truth and holiness prevail and reign in the body of Christ in Jesus name.

5. We pray for global harvest of souls and true revival in the body of Christ so as to be able to reach the unreached in Jesus name.

6. O Lord, send more faithful labourers and raise genuine ministers for your kingdom work in Jesus name.

7. O Lord, empower all the true ministers of the gospel and keep them from compromise and perils of the end time in Jesus name.

8. Let every weapon of darkness against the body of Christ and expansion of his kingdom on earth, be destroyed in Jesus name.

9. Holy Spirit of God, take over every activity of your Church on earth like the day of Pentecost in Jesus name.

10. O Lord God, keep FEIM till the end and let not the will and plan of Satan prevail over the Church, the set man, his family, the ministers and every member of the Ministry in Jesus name.

PRAYERS FOR NATION'S OR STATE'S

SCRIPTURES Isaiah 62 v 1 – 7; Ezekiel 8; Ezekiel 9; Daniel 9 v 15 – 22

EXHORTATION For the nation or State sake will I not hold my peace and for sake I will not rest, until the righteousness thereof go forth as brightness, and the salvation thereof, as a lamp that burneth. And the gentile shall see thy righteousness, and all kings thy glory, and thou shalt be called by a new name, which the wrath of the Lord shall name. Thou shalt also be a crown of glory in the hand of the Lord, and a royal diadem in the hand of thy God" (Isaiah 62 v 1 – 3).

PRAYERS "Pray for the peace of the nation or State, they shall prosper that love thee" Psalm 122 v 6

1. O Lord, touch and empower our leaders to fear you and to do what is right in Jesus name.

2. Let every wicked elders and evil youth, devising mischief and wicked counsels be put to shame and fade away in Jesus name.

3. Let all the wasters of human lives and resources in Nigeria be judged, exposed, disgraced and be wasted in Jesus name.

4. We reject bloodshed, flood and disasters henceforth in Nigeria in Jesus name.

5. Let every evil witchcraft, network, marine and occultic network over Nigeria be scattered and destroyed in Jesus name.

6. Let there be light and safety on our airways, waterways and road network in Jesus name.

7. O Lord, let your divine agenda override that of the evil agenda for Nigeria in Jesus name.

8. O Lord, raise intercessors for Nigeria and wake up the Church to pray in the name of Jesus.

9. O Lord, heal Nigeria and deliver her from the hand of the wicked powers, principalities and evil rulers in Jesus name.

10. (called out the nations or State) will manifest glory, I and my family will eat the good of the Land in Jesus name.

Faith Embassy International Ministries

(Revelation Church)
21 DAYS
FASTING & PRAYING
Manua

WEEK 1 JAN. 1ST - JAN. 7TH

1. Study the Bible passages, sing the songs of you have chosen, praise the Lord throughout the twenty-one days.

2. Break your fast at 3pm or 6pm as depending on your maturity in the Lord, prayers and health conditions.

3. Compulsory one-hour vigil between 12midnight – 1am daily.

4. Keep records of your dreams, visions and ask the Holy Spirit in accordance with John 14 v 26.

5. If you are not born again or you are not sure you are born again, pray these prayers before continuing: "O! Lord my father, I come unto you as a wretched sinner, have mercy on me, forgive me all of all my sins. Make me your child as from today. Write my name in the book of Life. Wash me clean with the blood of Jesus. Thank you my father for saving my soul. I declare that I am born again to the glory of God in the name of Jesus (John 3 v 16)

6. If you are discouraged, you are backsliding, perhaps your past is hunting you, receive the Grace of the Lord to repent of your past sins/habits now. Renounce them, ask God to take away from you any strange urge or taste for evil/defilement. Then ask the Holy Spirit to strengthen your inner man. (Ephesians 3 v 16)

7. Why you must pray and remain Holy always - Ps. 55 v 16; 17; Ps. 34 v 15 & 17; Ps. 65 v 2; 1 Pet. 1 v 15 - Without

holiness, your prayers will not be answered - Pray so that your joy can be full - Until you confront in prayers you cannot conquer - Pray to stop the enemies from stealing, killing and destruction - Prayers will hinder all the evil devices against you and your endeavour - The enemies do not grant freedom easily, you must get it by force. Mathew 11 v 12 - Breakthroughs are born in the womb of battles As you embark on this 21 days prayer and fasting program, God will visit you in an unusual way and empower you to recover all your past losses in the name of Jesus. IMPORTANT Get a copy of our Revelation Today DAILY DEVOTION For the year.

*Also subscribe for the early morning prophetic prayers Nehemiah 2, 4, 6; Ezra 4,5,6; Mathew 16 v 18 – 19; Jer. 1 v 1 – end; Col. 2 v 14-15; 1 Cor. 16 v 9; 2 Cor. 1 v 9 – 10 CONFESSION Psalm 50:15 "And call upon me in the day of trouble; I will deliver thee and thou shall glorify me"

PRAYERS

1.   Praise and worship unto the Lord for He is the Mighty man in charge of Faith Embassy International ministry
2.   Congregation and personal repentance to be carried out.
3.   Ask for mercy and grace, plead the blood of Jesus for cover you, your family and the Church
4.   Thank God on behalf of the Church on the following:

a. For founding the Ministry in the Power of the Holy Ghost

b. For His mercy, glory upon the Senior Pastor and his family

c. For how far God has helped you and the Ministry

d. For all the great testimonies since the inception of the Church

e. For frustrating the tokens of the liars and defeating our enemies.

f. For His revelation knowledge and anointing on the Ministry

g. For fulfilling His promise that He will build the Church and the gate of hell shall not prevail.

5. Rebuke and overthrow all Territorial Spirit (over the area where the Church is located) manifesting as

1. Occultism
2. Religious Deception
3. Prostitution

6. Command all Satanic Altars fashioned against the Church and other genuine ministries in the environment scatter by fire in Jesus name.

7. Every witchcraft and occultic stronghold against the Church, be pulled down in Jesus name.

8. Every witchcraft programme against you, be destroyed in Jesus name.

9. Every power using evil rosary, evil mat, evil incense, ritual, sacrifices against the Church die by fire in Jesus name.

10. Powers/Agents, using the sand to consult against the Church; Dust of the Earth, battle them to nothing in Jesus name.

11. Satanic agents, who have entered into covenant of death against the Church and her members die by your covenant in Jesus name.

12. Satanic vows, threats, plans against the progress of the Church and her members be nullified by the blood of Jesus in Jesus name.

13. Demonic campaign against the Church and her members be aborted in Jesus name.

14. Evil gathering, day and night against the Church and her members be scattered by the Rock of Ages, in Jesus name.

15. Powers that are making life difficult for the Church and her members swell up and burst to death in Jesus name.

16. Marine and Serpentine activities within the Church, be paralysed in Jesus name.

17. Marine and Witchcraft powers assigned to monitor the Church and her members, we anchor your heads to divine judgment in Jesus name.

18. Agents of darkness in any group within the Church be exposed and disgraced in Jesus name.

19. All the horses, chariots and their riders on assignment to cause evil in the Church, die on your assignment in Jesus name.

20. We decree confusion, futility, failure, miscalculation, spiritual accident to all agents of darkness sent to the Church and her members in Jesus name.

21. We decree harvesting of soul, vertical and horizontal growth in the Church in Jesus name.

22. We prophesy a higher anointing to destroy yokes, healing fire, mighty divine presence of God upon all our Church activities and members in Jesus name.

23. We command every door opened to agents of darkness in the Church)to be shut in Jesus name.

24. We paralyse satanic attacks against families, businesses of members, ministers and other workers in Jesus name.

25. Let the Fruit of the Spirit and the gift of the Spirit be in full operation in the Church day and night in Jesus name.

26. We decree DIVINE PROTECTION, DIVINE FAVOUR, DIVINE PROMOTION, Supernatural increase for the Church and all the members in Jesus name.

27. Our Church be mightily transformed to an ABODE OF UNUSUAL MIRACLES, a tent in the wilderness, a living spring in the desert for your generation in Jesus name.

28. The Church and her members.

•   No wall of resistance between you and God's visitation in Jesus name.

- Everything in creation will co-operate with you and serve you in Jesus name.

- Receive Prophetic and Apostolic Grace to affect your generation in Jesus name.

- Gates of creation are opened to you in Jesus name.

- Occultic Sanctions and Legislations over you are cancelled in Jesus name.

- You are released from the Mandates of Evil Altars in Jesus name.

- We shall by covenant serve God and make heaven in Jesus name.

- We receive a new level of GRACE and FAVOUR in Jesus name.

- The banner of God's Protection and Security is raised upon us in Jesus name.

- No evil traffic is permitted in your abode in Jesus name.

- Our Altar, Pew, Homes, Businesses, Children, Marriage shall not be desecrated in Jesus name.

- Our premises shall not be a habitation for evildoers; we will grow in purity in Jesus name.

- Our trees shall not be infested or contaminated in Jesus name.

- We shall fight like warriors and will always in Jesus name.

29. We receive the Grace to defend our salvation with fear and trembling, and to make heaven in Jesus name.

Jan 1: SHOW ME GREAT MERCY

O LORD SHOW ME GREAT MERCY SCRIPTURES Numbers 14 v 18; Psalm 57 v 10; Psalm 86 v 13; Psalm 103 v 11, 108 v 4; Eph. 2 v 4; Joshua 10 v 11 – 14; Judges 6 & 7; 2 Kings 4 v 1-7; Psalm 102 v 13; Roman 9 v 14 – 16; Acts 5 v 18 – 19 CONFESSION Psalm 86 v 13 – For great is thy mercy toward me: and thou hast delivered my soul from the lowest hell.

EXHORTATION Mercy is a gift from God. It is underserved. If it were not for God's mercy, we all would have faced terrible judgements long ago. If not for His mercy, He would have condemned us after our first offence. If not for His mercy, He would punish us each time we sin, but rather than letting us bear the full punishment for our sin, God demonstrated His mercy when He paid the penalty for our sin Himself. Psalm 6 v 2a – "Have mercy upon me O! Lord, for I am weak" is the heart felt cry of many. Some things will never yield good results unless God shows up with great mercy. When every other prayer has failed, the prayer of mercy never fails. The Lord God is the custodian of great mercy, no matter your level of sin or iniquity, when you run to God, He shows mercy. He alone has the prerogative of mercy.

- If God wants to judge mankind, none of us will be in existence now.

- God's mercy is always available not that we should take His mercies for granted.

- He gives us several opportunities to change our ways and turn a new leaf.

- God can show us great mercies than those received by our forefathers.

- The mercy of God is so great towards us, that we cannot measure it.

- No matter your situation now, what you need is the great mercy of God

- If prayer failed at any point in time, try thanksgiving, praise and worship, just begin to praise God, and begin to judge God faithful, even if you don't do it now, I know you will do it, Lord I am on your mercy list, envelop me with your cloud of great mercy. Note that God still sits on the mercy throne.

- It is the mercy of God that has kept our nation Nigeria intact, I pray the mercy of God will not leave us in Jesus name.

- Psalm 103 v 11 says great is the mercy of God towards them that fear Him.

- The mercy of God excels over judgement, even when people judge you, the great mercy of God over rides it.

- Great is the mercy of God, our God is rich in mercy, He is going to visit your case today in Jesus name.

• I pray for you, wherever God directs you, His great mercy will accompany you in Jesus name.

• As you procure that visa letter, you need the mercy of God to succeed.

• With your anointing you need the mercy of God to achieve good success, it is the mercy of God that breaths His grace over you. I pray that the Grace of God will rest upon your anointing in Jesus name.

WHEN DO YOU NEED THE GREAT MERCY OF GOD

1. When you are in a complete mess

2. When it seems your vision is bigger than you.

3. When you are below the ground level on any matter.

4. When you are an executive beggar.(Educated but begging to survive)

5. When you have been totally condemned in the court of man, in fact they have said nothing good will come out of your Nazareth.

6. When all hope seems lost and you feel like giving up, in fact you are suicidal now, don't be discouraged, the great mercy of God will locate you in Jesus name.

7. When no man can answer your questions.

8. When you are frustrated beyond description, in fact you cannot describe it. Your frustration is killing, shocking, stifling, chocking, unexplainable, embarrassing, messy and even challenging your salvation.

9. When you are swimming in the ocean of failure and embarrassment

10. When men lied against you and no one believes you.

11. When you get demoted, instead of being promoted.

12. When everything around you fails.

13. When you are to meet an important deadline and your strength is failing. i.e deadline panic.

14. When it seems age is no longer on your side.

15. When it seems eyes are not on you anymore i.e. people don't fancy you anymore.

16. When all your age mates have achieved and you are still behind.

17. When people are saying nothing good can happen to you.

18. When you are desperate to take a foolish step because of frustration.

19. When you have been written off by friends, family members and close allies.

20. When you feel no helper can locate you. It is my prayer that the great mercy of the Almighty God will bring

something good out of you, and bring out your testimonies in Jesus name.

1. Elizabeth – her neighbour and cousins heard of the great mercy shown to her and they rejoiced with her. Luke 1 v 57 - 58

2. Joseph was shown mercy that MADE him in life. He became notable in life by the great mercy of God. Gen. 39 v 21

3. Solomon reiterated the fact that God showed David his father great mercy, by making him have a son on the throne in Israel. 2 Chronicles 1 v 8

4. Daughter of Abraham - Luke 13 v 11 – 17

5. The man born blind - John 9 v 1 – 7

6. Jeremiah regained his freedom – Jeremiah 40 v 1 – 4 7. Daniel in the lions den - Daniel 6 v 16 – 23

8. The Shinammite Woman, gift of a son, and the raising afterwards of the son from the dead. 2 Kings 4 v 14 – 37

HINDERANCES TO GOD'S GREAT MERCY

2 Cor. 6 v 14 – 16

1. Deliberate sin

2. Keeping accursed/demonic materials

3. Using false measures

4. Engaging in illegal businesses

5. Taking bribe/graft

6. Unforgivenness, malice, wrath, envy etc.

7. Evil speaking

8. Robbery

9. Venerating the dead

10. Idolatry

11. Improper dressing

12. Wickedness

13. Sexual Immorality

14. Ungodly living

15. Fraud

16. Perversion of justice

17. Robbing God of tithes, offerings etc.

18. Rebellion and Disobedience

19. Patronizing fake prophets

20. Abortion

21. Greed.

ACTIVATES OF GOD'S GREAT MERCY

1. Be born-again - John 3 v 3

2. Get sanctified and filled with the Holy Ghost – Acts 1 v 4 – 5

3. Live a life of holiness - 1 Peter 1 v 15

4. Live a life of total obedience – Deut. 28 v 1, Isaiah 1 v 1 – 19

5. Live a life of absolute surrender and total yieldedness – Galatian 2 v 20

6. Be kingdom-minded always – 1 Peter 4 v 7

7. Give faithfully – i.e tithes, first fruits, kingdom project, seed etc.

8. Intercede for others, be a burden bearer – Luke 6 v 38

9. Remember the widows, orphans and the less privileged

10. Don't be logical with God and interfere with the laws and principles of God. Malachi 3 v 8 – 12 . The foolishness of God is wiser than men, always remember 1 Cor. 1 v 25

11. Shun a sinful lifestyle - Jer. 5 v 25 12. Avoid bitterness, wrath, anger, clamour, malice, envy etc. Eph. 4 v 26 – 31

13. Be diligent in your work - Heb. 6 v 12, Proverbs 18 v 9 – God will not remember a lazy person.

14. Don't go to Egypt for help, depend on the Lord absolutely – Prov. 16 v 2 & 3; Isaiah 31 v 1 & 2 15. Let the

fear of God rule your life – Prov. 19 v 23 16. Learn to give thanks always – 1 Thess 5 v 18 Blind Bartimaeus asked for mercy before asking for his eyes to be opened, Mark 10 v 46 – 52.

A prayer of desperation must be preceded by a cry for mercy. As you call on God, His great mercy shall locate you in Jesus name.

PRAYERS

1. From every evil yoke, I receive my freedom by God's mercy in Jesus name.

2. From every hard yoke of bondage in Jesus name, I receive my freedom, by the mercy of God

3. Periodic warfare from the pit of hell attacking my breakthrough by the mercy of God be aborted in Jesus name.

5. Dream attacks swallowing my blessing, I command by God's mercy be cancelled in Jesus name.

6. Mercy of God lift me up in Jesus name.

7. Lamentation 3 v 17 – any evil word from the mouth of men against my life, mercy of God, cancel them in Jesus name.

8. At the junction of confusion, mercy of God, bail me out in Jesus name.

9. From every ocean of failure, mercy of God, bail me out in Jesus name.

10. O Lord, show me great mercy in Jesus name.

11. Great mercy of God, locate me in Jesus name.

12. By the great mercy of God, O Lord, restore my departed glory in Jesus name.

13. By the great mercy of God, all my captured blessings, be released in Jesus name.

15. By the great mercy of God, my positive dreams, manifest in Jesus name.

16. By the great mercy of God, O Lord, deliver me from evil burdens in Jesus name.

17. By the great mercy of God, all my pending breakthroughs, manifest in Jesus name.

18. By the great mercy of God, all my benefits in chains, be loosed in Jesus name.

19. By the great mercy of God, doors of opportunities, be opened unto me in Jesus name.

20 By the great mercy of God, my book of remembrance, be opened in Jesus name.

21 By the great mercy of God, O Lord raise me up to the next level in Jesus name.

22 By the great mercy of God, all anti-progress altars erected against me, scatter in Jesus name.

23 By the great mercy of God, my life/destiny, be withdrawn from any evil control in Jesus name.

24 By the great mercy of God, anointing of the overcomer, fall on me in Jesus name.

25 By the great mercy of God, anointing to possess my possessions fall on me in Jesus name.

JAN 2: TAKE OVER

OH LORD, TAKE OVER! SCRIPTURES Exo. 2 v 23 – 25; 2 Chro. 20 v 14 & 15; Ps. 55 v 22; John 6 v 37; Luke 5 v 1; Exo. 14 v 14; Exo. 23 v 22; Ps.105 v 14 & 15; Zech. 2 v 8; Ps 46:1; 1 Sam. 17:49 – 50;; Ex. 11:1; Exo. 15:9 – 10; Exo. 15:23; Exo. 17:14; Exo. 23:20; Deut. 7:15; Deut. 28:12; Joshua 5:9 CONFESSION 1 Sam. 2:9b "For by strength shall no man prevail. Ps. 127:1 says "Except the Lord build the house, they labour in vain that built it. Except the Lord keep the city, the watchman waketh but in vain" O! Lord my father, I surrender this situation (mention it) unto you, take over from me. I have put my trust and hope in you and I know I shall not be stranded. By your help Lord! Let my destiny meet with your favour that I may enter into your goodness in Jesus name.

EXHORTATION Before God can take over any situation in our lives, we must forgive everyone who has offended us. What is it to forgive? Matt 6 v 9 – 13; Eph. 4 v 26 - 32

• To forgive means to stop feeling angry with somebody who has done something to harm, annoy or to upset you.

• Forgiveness is allowing God the exclusive right to JUDGE or CORRECT.

• Forgiveness brings FREEDOM and PEACE to you.

• An offence you keep becomes a FENCE between you and God.

• Since God has forgiven us, let's forgive others.

SOME BIBLICAL CASES

1. In the beginning the earth was void, no form and there was darkness. God took over, the Spirit of God moved. He started by creating light against darkness, water, herbs trees, moon and stars, earth and finally the man on the 6th day. - Gen. 1

2. When the children of Israel cried to God in bondage, He heard their cry and took over. He arranged for a deliverer, Moses. He got his attention through the burning bush encounter. Exodus. 3 v 2.

3. When God takes over, he arranges for an escape beyond your imagination.

4. At Pharaoh's Palace, God took over. Exodus. 7 v 10 & 12 and Aaron's rod turned to snake. Exodus. 7 v 20 - River turned to Blood; Exodus. 8 v 6 - Frogs came out of the waters; Exodus. 8 v 15 - Dusts became lice. When God takes over, the finger of God will appear to stop any form of manipulation.

5 At the Red Sea, Exodus. 14 v 21; God took over and the Red Sea parted. The ransomed passed through again and God took over. v 25 The water returned and covered Pharaoh and the chariots and the enemies. When God takes over at your Red sea Exodus. 14 v 14 - The Lord shall fight for you and you shall hold your peace.

6. At Jordan, he took over and at Jericho he took over. Joshua 3 v 14 – 17

7. Bitter Marah water sweetened. (Sorrow to Joy) Exodus. 15 v 23 – 25.

8. Daily Manna sent (Except on Sabbath day)

Exodus. 16 v 14 – 35

9. Nadab & Abihu consumed for offering strange fire (Vengeance) Exodus. 17 v 5 – 7

10. Earth swallowed Dathan, Korah & Abiram (Vengeance) Numbers. 16 v 3

11. Wall of Jericho fell down (Obstruction removed) - Joshua 6 v 6 – 20

12. Iron ax-head made to swin (Recovery) - II Kings 6 v 5 – 7

13. Shadrach, Meshach and Abednego delivered from the furnance - Daniel. 3 v 19 – 27

14. Daniel saved in the den of lions (Deliverance) - Daniel. 6 v 16 – 23

15. Impotent man cured at the pool of Bethesda (Healing) John 5 v 1 – 9

16. Lazarus raised from the dead at Bethany (Restoration) John 11 v 38 - 44

17. The Outpouring of the Holy Spirit with signs following. (Power outpouring) - Acts 2

18. Lame man at the beautiful gate (Hope Restored) - Acts 3

19. Angels opened the prison gates (Angelic Assistance) - Acts 5 20. Paul unharmed by the viper (Safety) - Acts 28 v 3 – 5

WHEN GOD TAKES OVER

1. He makes your past a History for tomorrow's testimonies

2. He changes your level/position/status

3. He makes impossibilities possible

4. He removes all obstacles

5. He levels all mountains and their builders

6. He confronts your stubborn Goliath

7. He gives you Honey out of the rock and not from the stringing bees. 8. He takes over and fights your battles

9. He gives you directions and back up

10. He delivers you from the powers of darkness.

11. He makes you great, and increases your greatness Ps. 71 v 21, Gen 12 v 2, Jer. 30V19

12. He heals your medically written off diseases.

13. He takes away your shame and reproach Jer. 33 v 6; Isa. 62 v 1 – 5.

14. He empowers you to become what he has ordained you to be. Deut 8 v 18.

15. He restructures, re-organises you completely.

16. He touches all the department of your life and gives you values because anything God touches has values. 17. He brings you out of Horrible Pits - Ps. 140

18. He makes your Mess a Message

19. He makes you to Arise, Stand and Shine.

20. He gives you a new beginning.

21. He protects, preserves, provides for you.

22. He changes your story and makes your life a WONDER no matter your background.

23. He makes your enemies tremble before you.

24. He daily loads you with benefits

25. He barricades your life with the wall of protection, joy and happiness.

FOR GOD TO TAKE OVER

1. Surrender your life at His Invitation - John 3 v 3

2. Get sanctified and filled with Holy Ghost - Acts 1 v 4 & 5

3. Live a life of Holiness - 1 Pet. 1 v 15

4. Live a life of Obedience - Deut. 28 v 1; Isa. 1 v 19

5. Get to know him daily personally, Quiet time - Eph. 1 v 17 – 19

6. Live a life of absolute Surrender and total yield to God. Gal. 2 v 20.

7. Visit Calvary regularly for purging - Col. 3 v 1.

8. Be heavenly minded always - 1 Pet. 4 v 7

PRAYER

1. O Lord, take over my life affairs in Jesus name.

2. O Lord, wherever I have failed, take over in Jesus name.

3. O Lord, wherever I am helpless and confused, take over in Jesus name.

4. O Lord, whenever I need urgent help, take over in Jesus name.

5. O Lord, wherever I need a touch of healing, take over in Jesus name.

6. O Lord, in any way I need provision, take over in Jesus name.

7. O Lord, wherever my family needs your settlement, take over in Jesus name.

8. O Lord, in any area I must be restored take over in Jesus name.

9. Concerning

- My wife and children, O Lord take over

- My work and project, O Lord take over

- My expectations, O Lord take over

- My finances, O Lord take over

- My spiritual growth, O Lord take over

- My tomorrow, O Lord take over

- My progress, O Lord take over

10. O Lord, by your power, make my life a wonder in Jesus name.

11. O Lord, empower me for a new beginning in Jesus name.

12. O Lord, take over destiny to give my life a meaning in Jesus name.

13. Holy Father, by your great power take my destiny out of horrible pit in Jesus name.

14. O Lord, let your finger arise and stop all manipulation in my life in Jesus name.

15. Almighty God, let not my life go the way enemy wanted it in Jesus name.

16. O Lord, let not the wicked prevail over me in Jesus name.

17. My father, let my angel of testimonies locate me in Jesus name. 18. I shall laugh last in Jesus name.

19. O Lord, let your power of fulfilment possess my life in Jesus name.

20. O Lord, Glorify yourself in my life in Jesus name. Amen.

JAN 3: REMEMBER ME

O LORD, REMEMBER ME. SCRIPTURES Genesis 9 v 11 – 15; Exo. 2 v 23 – 25; 2 Sam. 11 v 20; 1 Chro. 4 v 9 v 10; Isaiah 43 v 18 v 19; Luke 1 v 11 – 16; Gen. 41 v 14 – 46; 1 Sam. 1 v 5 – 20; 2 Samuel 9 v 1 – 13; Esther 6 v 1 - 12

EXHORTATION Beloved, when you and I are forgotten by men, there is a God who keeps account of everything we do, who has not forgotten us. In the Bible, the likes of Joseph, Hannah, Mephibosheth and Mordecai were forgotten but God remembered them at the right time and they received God's reward much greater than what this world could have given. From the Scriptures, we can see that God has plans for all His children and His plans are good.

The purpose of God for us is not to be stagnant or to remain ordinary all through life. It is up to us to tap into His promises and appropriate them to enjoy His faithfulness. There are times we need to pray and fast for Him to remember us, it my prayer that God will remember us for good in Jesus name.

God must remember you so that the underlisted will come to pass in your life: - To fulfil your destiny - Jeremiah 29 v 11; John 10 v 10 - To turn your shame to fame - Zeph. 3 v 19 - To be fruitful in all ways - Zech. 8 v 12 - To move from prison to the palace - Gen. 41 v 14 – 44 - To be celebrated in your life – Mal. 3 v 16-18 - To bring your expectation to pass – Prov. 23 v 18 - To enjoy your life with ease and comfort – Job 36 v 11; Isa 1 v 19 - To be a blessing to your generation - Gen. 12 v 2 - To be the head and not the tail - Deut. 28 v 13 Beloved, when God remembers you do not forget God, pay your vow and also remember those God used for you. When God remembers you, there will be abundance of life, fulfilment of promises, honour, glory, miracles and God's deliverance. As you lift up your eyes to your maker in prayers, He will surely remember you in Jesus name.

PRAYERS

1. Lord, remember me and let the whole world know that you are God in Jesus name.

2. Father, remember my service in your house and remember me in Jesus name.

3. Lord, remember me and show up in my situation in Jesus name.

4. Lord, remember me by your mercy in Jesus name.

5. Lord, remember me and give me victory over my enemies in Jesus name.

6. Father, remember me and make a partaker of your goodness this year in Jesus name.

7. Father, remember me and lift me up beyond my imaginations in Jesus name.

8. In the name of Jesus, my ordained helpers will remember.

9. This year will be a year of manifestation of God's greatness in my life in Jesus name.

10. Thank you Lord for remembering me for good in Jesus name.

JAN 4: OPEN MY EYES

O LORD, OPEN MY EYES. SCRIPTURES 2 Kings 6:8 – 20; Proverbs 20: 24 & 27; Jer. 33:3; Deut. 29:29; Dan. 2:22; Ps. 58; Ps. 25:14; Eph. 1: 17 & 18; Ezek. 1: 1 – 3; Luke 24: 30 & 31; Psalm 119 v 18; 2 Kings 6 v 8 – 20; Proverbs 20 v 24 & 27; Jer. 33 v 3; Deut. 29 v 29; Dan. 2 v 22

EXHORTATION The Psalmist in Psalm 119 v 18 cried to God to open his eyes so that he can see wondrous things which ordinary eyes cannot see. His physical eyes were opened, yet he realised that he was not seeing everything that was supposed to be seen. He observed that his spiritual vision was blocked. His prayer was basically asking God to give him an understanding, enlighten his mind and for God to allow the scales to drop from his eyes so that he could discern divine and spiritual things. Please confess this: 'The Blood of Jesus sanctify my eyes to see beyond the physical in Jesus name:

My eyes shall not be dark, manipulated, partially or totally blinded in the name of Jesus. I receive the gift of vision and deep dreams in Jesus name. I confess that no spiritual cataract or glaucoma will affect my inner eyes in Jesus name. The Lord will grant me access to information clearly for I see through the eyes of God.' As you seek His face in prayer, He will open your eyes to secrets that you must know for you to prosper and live in good health throughout this year and beyond in Jesus name.

PRAYERS

1. Thank God for the Holy Spirit who will open your spiritual eyes

2. Lord give me the spirit of revelation in Jesus name. 3. Lord remove spiritual cataract from my eyes in Jesus name.

4. Lord my father, deliver me from spiritual laziness in Jesus name.

5. O! Lord, teach me and reveal deep and secret things in Jesus name.

6. O! Lord, open my eyes to the secrets I need to know about my foundation in the name of Jesus.

7. O! Lord let every veil preventing me from seeing visions be removed in Jesus name.

8. O! Lord reveal your mind for the new the new year in Jesus name.

9. O! Lord make me a vessel capable of knowing your secrets in Jesus name. 10. I bind every demon that may want to pollute my spiritual antenna in Jesus name.

JAN 5: KEEP ME HOLY

OH LORD KEEP ME HOLY IN JESUS NAME SCRIPTURES Oba 1:17, Psm 110:3, Psm 93:5, 1 Chr16:29, Jer 2:3, Luk 1:75, Rom 1:4, Eph 4:24, 1 Ths 4:7, Heb 12:14, Exo 30:29, Num 6:5, Rom 11:16, Eph 5:27, Rev 22:11, Lev 20:7, 1 Pet 1:15-16, Psm 96:9, Num 15:40, 1 Ths 3:13, 1 Cor 15:10

EXHORTATION In Heb 12:14 the Bible says "Follow peace with all men, and holiness, without which no man shall see the Lord." This implies that holiness is a requirement for having a lasting encounter with God and experiencing a higher dimension of supernatural intervention in your affairs. Christianity without holiness is reduced to a life of struggles and hardships. The subject of holiness is essential to the life of a Christian. With holiness comes the power to possess your possession. Obadiah 1:17 says "Upon mount Zion shall be deliverance, and there shall be holiness; and the house of Jacob shall possess their possessions." Deliverance cannot be long sustained without a life of holiness In 1 Pet 1:15-16 the Apostle Peter admonishes "As He who hath called you is holy, so be ye holy in all manner of conversation; because it is written, be ye holy; for I am holy." Becoming holy is an almost impossible task which no man can accomplish in the energy of the flesh. That is why a cry for God's grace is essential in order to live holy and to possess all your possessions this year. You will make it in Jesus name

PRAYERS

1. Thank God for the gift of life

2. Ask for forgiveness of sins by the mercy of God

3. Plead the blood of Jesus for your purification

4. O Lord my God, empower me to operate by the fear of God in holiness and consecration unto You in Jesus name

5. Any character deficiency that will not allow me to live holy this year, be destroyed by fire in Jesus name

6. O Lord my Father grant me grace me to live holy throughout this year and beyond in Jesus name

7. According to Zec 3:1-4, oh Lord remove the garment of filthiness from me and clothe me with the garment of holiness in Jesus name

8. Any foundational covenant tying me down to sin, break by fire in Jesus name

9. Anointing of holiness, fall upon me in Jesus name

10. O Lord my God, keep me holy in Jesus name

JAN 6: STEP INTO MY MATTER

OH LORD STEP INTO MY MATTER IN JESUS NAME
SCRIPTURES 1 Thessalonians 5:17, Isa 6:7, Jeremiah
33:9, Zephaniah 3:20, Jeremiah 29:11, Matthew 14:24-33,
James 5:16, Luke 18:1, Phillipians 2:9-10, 1 Samuel 2:1-2,
Psalm 121:1-8,

EXHORTATION

Make this confession out loud: "Psalm 121:1-8 I will lift
up mine eyes unto the hills from where comes my help. My
help comes from the Lord who made heaven and earth. He
will not suffer my foot to be moved, He that keeps me will
not slumber, Behold, he that keeps my Israel shall neither
sleep nor slumber. The Lord is my keeper; the Lord is my
shade upon my right hand. He shall preserve my going out
and my coming in from this time forth and even
forevermore (Amen)" Psalm 126:1 "When the Lord turned
again the captivity of Zion we were like them that dream"
When God steps into your matter, your overnight weeping
will turn to joy in the morning; your captivity will turn to
laughter and rejoicing; your obstacle will turn to miracles
and your trials will turn to triumphs in Jesus name.

It does not matter how long you have been oppressed by
the enemies or buffeted by contrary situations and negative
winds, the moment God steps into your situation the storms
of your life will cease in Jesus name. Every negative
situation must bow because God has highly exalted Christ

and has given Him a name which is above every other name, that at the name of Jesus, every knee must bow, of the things in heaven, things on earth and things beneath the earth. Philippians 2:9-10. Any power assigned to attack you with strange problems shall bow to the name of Jesus as He steps into that matter in the name of Jesus. As long as you can pray to God ceaselessly for your needs in righteousness, God will definitely step into your matter in Jesus name. The man who can pray has nothing to fear. The key that changes God's promises to reality is fervent prayers James 5:16b. As you pray, the Lord will step into your matter and bring you into realms of unending rejoicing in Jesus name

PRAYERS

1. O Lord, by your mercy and power step into my life and remove every stubborn problem destroying good things in my life every month and every year in Jesus name.

2. O Lord, my Father, correct every wrong step I have taken that has brought problems into my life in Jesus name.

3. O Lord, my father, step into my matter and let all invisible handcuffs preventing my hands from receiving blessing, break by fire in Jesus name.

4. Hosts of heaven, step into all my matters throughout this year in Jesus name

5. By the blood of Jesus, my head and my hand, reject failure, poverty, amputated blessings accidents and bewitchment in Jesus name

6. O strong arm of the Lord, deliver me from the yoke of wickedness in Jesus name

7. By divine intervention, Lord step into my health and bring me perfect healing in Jesus Name

8. O Lord, by your mercy step into my health to bring perfect healing in Jesus name Jer 17:14

9. My internal and external organs, reject evil deposit, in Jesus name Holy Spirit of God step into my matter and cause every storm to cease in my life in Jesus name

JAN. 7: **FAVOUR ME**

O GOD, FAVOUR ME IN JESUS NAME SCRIPTURES
Deut. 7:7-8, Exo 3:21-22, Job 42:10, Esther 2:9, Esther 5:2, Luke 1:5- end, Gen 41:14, Luke 5:1-10, Pro 3:1-4, Job 33:26, Psalm 30:1-end (Note vs5 & 6), Rom 8:1-end, Luke 2:52, Job 10:12, Gen 18:17, Act 7:46, Psalm 102:13, Dan 1:9, Act 7:10, Pro 18:22, Exo 3:21-22

EXHORTATION

Favour is an act of kindness from God to man and from man to man. Favour is goodwill from God to man. Deut 7:7-8. It is a divine help to the one who is less fortunate. When the favour of God is in place everything will work to your advantage which will generate a glorious future because God makes everything to work together for your good. The operation of God's favour in any man's life is the guarantee of a glorious future. Those who triumph in God's kingdom do so by the favour of God at work in them. The favour of God will overwhelm you throughout this year in Jesus name Favour is a demonstration of the compassion of God towards the less fortunate people. It is an expression of God's love and kindness. Favour justifies you for greatness; it is an expression of love to us as the people of God. Psalm 5:12 says "For thou, LORD, wilt bless the righteous; with favour wilt thou compass him as with a shield" Favour is a supernatural shield from hardship and shame. By the favour of God shame will be far from you this year in Jesus name.

Unveiled Faces - 78

Until favour shows up, delay continues; stagnation prevails. From now on delay and stagnation cease to exist in your life in Jesus name. Favour enables the throne of your destiny to be established such as it did in the lives of Joseph, Esther, David and even Jesus Christ Luke 2:52. When the favour of God comes upon you, it stirs the heart of man to favour you. This year will be your year of supernatural favour in Jesus mighty name. Pray the following prayers with faith in your heart

PRAYER

Sing this song: Favour me Baba favour me favour me Holy Spirit favour me

1. Plead the blood of Jesus over your life, family, business and career in Jesus name

2. Any foundational power assigned to hinder the flow of favour in my life, die by fire in Jesus name

3. O Lord my father, anchor my life and destiny to unexplainable favour in Jesus name

4. Witchcraft cobwebs preventing my life from receiving favour, be roasted by fire in Jesus name

5. My head reject delay, stagnation and shame in Jesus name.

6. O Lord my Father, let the current of your favour flow into my life in Jesus name

7. Anointing of favour, fall on me in Jesus name

8. Among the multitude, favour of God will single me out in Jesus name

9. Wherever I go, the light of God's favour will shine on me in Jesus name

10. O Lord, my Father, clothe my destiny, work and family with your mantle of favour in Jesus name

WEEK 2 JAN. 8Th - 14TH

1.When we walk with the Lord, in the light of His Word What a glory He sheds on our way While we do His good will He abides with us still And with all who will trust and obey Chorus: Trust and obey, for there is no other way To be happy in Jesus, but to trust and obey

2. Not a shadow can rise, Not a cloud in the skies But His smile quickly drives it away Not a doubt nor a fear Not a sigh nor a tear Can abide while we trust and obey.

3. Not a burden we bear, Not a sorrow we share But our toil He doth richly repay Not a grief nor a loss Not a frown nor a cross But is blest if we trust and obey

4. But we never can prove, The delights of His love Until all on the altar we lay For the favour He shows And the joy He bestows Are for them who will trust and obey

5. Then in fellowship sweet, We will sit at His feet Or we'll walk by His side in the way What He says we will do Where He sends we will go Never fear, only trust and obey

WEEKLY CONFESSION SCRIPTURE

- Ephesian 3 v 20 - "Now unto him that is able to do exceeding abundantly above all that we ask or thing, according to the power that worketh in us"

1. God will remember me, my family and work for good this year in Jesus name.

2. Anointing for pleasant surprises, fall on me this year in Jesus name.

3. I receive directions and New ideas from God in Jesus name.

4. Any step I take according to the will of God shall lead to success in Jesus name.

5. All my impossibilities shall be made possible in Jesus name.

6. Doors of New things shall be opened unto me and my family in Jesus name.

7. The Lord shall exceed my expectations this year in Jesus name.

JAN 8: I REJECT REPEATED PROBLEMS

I REJECT REPEATED PROBLEMS SCRIPTURES Isaiah 19 v 3; Proverbs 18 v 10; Isaiah 3 v 10; Acts 12 v 1 – 8; Jeremiah 40 v 1 – 4

EXHORTATION Beloved, the scripture in Isaiah 19 v 3 says "The spirit of Egypt shall fail in the midst thereof and I will destroy the counsel thereof: and they shall seek to the idols, and to the charmers, and to them that have familiar spirits, and to the wizards" The spirit of Egypt is the spirit of bondage, oppression, spirit of poverty, limitation etc. These are the spirits that foster repeated problems in the life of man, but God says these spirits shall fail and you shall receive your deliverance in Jesus name. Repeating circular problems can be frustrating leading to maddening oppression.

In Acts 12 v 1 – 8, Apostle Peter was imprisoned by authorities because it pleased a particular set of people, but prayers were said for him by the Church, that is why you must not joke with prayers. A night prior to Apostle Peter being executed he had an angelic visitation, where chains used to bind him fell off. God intervened divinely and rescued him. That same God is still alive and He will deliver you from every repeated problems in Jesus name. As you pray these warfare prayers, the battle of repeated problems will terminate in Jesus name and there shall be progress in all areas of your life in Jesus name.

PRAYERS

1. Enemies rejoicing at any repeated problems in my life, be disgraced in Jesus name.

2. Chains of darkness holding me down to where I don't like and causing repeated problems in my life, I command you to break in the name of Jesus.

3. Chains of darkness holding me down to ling time problems/repeated problems/wrong position and horrible experiences, break in Jesus name.

4. Unknown covenants that have chained me down to the same spot over the years, causing embarrassing situations, break by fire in Jesus name.

5. Chains of darkness tying me down to diseases, barrenness, delay and stagnation, break in Jesus name.

6. Foundational controversy surrounding my turn-around, blood of Jesus kill them in Jesus name.

7. Circle of repeated problems in my life, break in Jesus name.

8. Demonic oaths, covenants/agreements re-enforcing problems in my life, blood of Jesus cancels them in Jesus name.

9. Every curse of lack of progress operating in my life, break in Jesus name.

10. Nahum 1 v 9 - I decree afflictions will not rise again in my life in Jesus name.

JAN. 9: I REJECT STAGNATION

I REJECT STAGNATION IN JESUS NAME Deut. 1 v 6 – 7; 2 Kings 7 v 3 – 5; 8 – 9; Proverbs 23 v 5; Hosea 9 v 11; John 5 v 1 – 9; Psalm 17 v 6 – 13; Jeremiah 32 v 27 – 28

EXHORTATION

Beloved, I want you to pray this prayer before we go further. "O Lord my God, remove my name from the register of stagnation in the name of Jesus. The subject of stagnation must be handled with utmost seriousness, seeing the way it is devastating lives, organisations and families, making the people of God everywhere to cry out bitterly for help. Stagnation is a dark evil force. It keeps one on the same spot ridiculously. When it sets in, every forward movement and progress is crippled.

CAUSES OF STAGNATION

a. Living without a purpose in life.

b. Mistakes and errors

c. Lack of ordained divine helpers. John 5 v 1 – 8

d. Pessimistic attitude towards life

e. Procrastination

f. Keeping wrong company - 1 Cor. 15 v 33

g. Sinful lifestyle - Jeremiah 5 v 25 The above causes are just to mention few. Search your life and see if you fall in any of the listed causes. Work on them and be determined to move forward in life, live a better and improved life and God will help you in Jesus name. As you pray these prayers every form of stagnation in your life will disappear in Jesus name.

PRAYERS

1. Spirit of stagnation, I bind you in the name of Jesus.

2. Spirit of stagnation, I curse you to the roots in the name of Jesus.

3. Every yoke of stagnation, disturbing my life, scatter by fire in Jesus name.

4. Every arrow of stagnation fired at my progress, backfire in the name of Jesus.

5. Every garment of stagnation I am wearing unknowingly, catch fire in Jesus name.

6. Satanic padlock of stagnation working against my progress, break by fire in the name of Jesus.

7. Any evil concrete that has bound me to the same spot over the years, scatter by thunder in Jesus name.

8. Anything responsible for stagnation in my life, be removed and die in Jesus name.

9. Every strongman delegated against my work to cause stagnation, die, in Jesus name.

10. Every serpent of stagnation biting my work, die by fire in the name of Jesus.

JAN. 10: I REJECT SICKNESS

I REJECT SICKNESS IN JESUS NAME SCRIPTURES
Exodus 23 v 25; Isaiah 53 v 3 – 5; Exodus 15 v 26;
Jeremiah 17 v 14; 1 Peter 2 v 24

EXHORTATION

Sicknesses and diseases are of the devil. 1 John 3 v 8b
says "For this purpose, the son of God was manifested, that
He might destroy the works of the devil" I command
sicknesses and diseases ravaging your life to be destroyed
in Jesus name. Divine health is the exclusive preserve of the
redeemed of God. As a child of God, whenever your
physical body is weak you have been authorised to
command it to receive the strength of God. Scripture says
"let the weak say, I am strong" In the name of Jesus I
command strength of the Lord to take over in every area of
weakness in your body. According to James 5 v 15 "the
prayer of faith shall save the sick, and the Lord shall raise
him up" By the power in the blood of Jesus let your body
rise up from the bed of languishing in Jesus name. Every
fountain of sickness in your body I command it to dry up in
the name of Jesus.

PRAYERS

1. By your mercy O Lord, deliver my body from
sicknesses in Jesus name.

2. Thou healing power of God, flow through my life and remove every sickness in Jesus name.

3. Every dream of sickness that wants to manifest at all cost, be cancelled by the blood of Jesus.

4. Blood of Jesus, flow into my mortal body and remove every sickness and disease in Jesus name.

5. Balm of Gilead, flow into my life in Jesus name.

6. Every stronghold of sickness ravaging my life, be destroyed by fire in Jesus name.

7. According to Nahum 1 v 9 affliction will not rise again the second time in Jesus name.

8. Every yoke of sickness and diseases upon my life, break by the anointing of the Holy Spirit in Jesus name.

9. O Lord my God, command deliverance upon my life from sicknesses and diseases in Jesus name. 10. Anointing of God for healing, flow into my life in Jesus name.

JAN. 11: I REJECT SUDDEN BAD NEW OR DEATH

I REJECT SUDDEN DEATH IN JESUS NAME
SCRIPTURES John 10:28 – 30; Psalm 91; Romans. 5:10; Psalm 105:14 – 15; Psalm 34 – 7; Psalm 23; Job 5:26; Psalm 118:17; Isaiah 65:22; Psalm 92:12, 14; Psalm 91; Proverbs. 9:11; Deuteronomy 4:40; Ps. 140:4 & 7;

EXHORTATION

Throughout this year and beyond, sudden death is not your portion in the name of Jesus. Psalm 91 v 7 says "a thousand shall fall at your side and ten thousand at thy right hand; but it shall not come near you" Throughout this year death will be far from you and your family in Jesus name. Every programme of death, every proclamation of death, every prophesy of death, every prediction of death, every agenda of death shall not prosper in your life in the name of Jesus. I decree that anyone planning sudden death for you and your family members shall fall by the way side and die, and the foxes shall eat them up in Jesus name. (Psalm 63 v 10)

PRAYERS

1. Thank God for the power over death through our Lord Jesus Christ.

2. I release my destiny from the hold of sudden death in Jesus name.

3. All attempts of sudden death made against me, be aborted in Jesus name.

4. Arrows of untimely death fired into my life, backfire by Holy Ghost fire to the senders in Jesus name.

5. I withdraw my name and that of my family from the register of untimely death in Jesus name.

6. Satanic graves dug for me and my family, swallow your diggers in Jesus name.

7. Every satanic carpenter constructing coffin of sudden death for me and my family, be buried in your own coffin in Jesus name.

8. My life will not be aborted before my God ordained time in Jesus name.

9. Every dream of sudden death tormenting my life and that of my family members, be cancelled by the blood of Jesus in Jesus name.

10. Covenant of sudden death cutting people's destinies short in my family be broken in Jesus name (Isaiah 28 v 18)

JAN. 12: I REJECT NEGATIVE PRAYERS

I REJECT NEGATIVE PRAYERS IN JESUS NAME SCRIPTURES Acts 23 v 12-27, Psalm 2 v 1-4, Numbers 22 v 4-21, Numbers 23 v1 - 23, 1Samuel. 17 v 43-46, Psalm 109 v 28, Isaiah 47 v 12-13; Isaiah 54 v 17; Psalm 55 v 5 – 16; Job 36 v 15 – 18

EXHORTATION

Beloved, negative prayers implies negative thoughts, imaginations, decree, confession, declaration, curses and pronouncement, but I pray for you that any negative statement and pronouncement issued against you and your family shall be aborted in Jesus name. The heart of man is desperately wicked who can know it? Jeremiah 17 v 9. May the Lord separate your life and destiny from those who are wishing you evil on a daily basis in Jesus name. There are people whose imaginations and prayers against you is just for them to hear that you have fallen from the Zenith of life or you have fallen into mistakes and errors.

Their hearts are imagining it and their mouth are praying same but Job 5 v 12 says that the Lord will disappoint them. David said there is violence in their tongues, deceit and guile resides in their mouth, for it was not an enemy far away that rose up against me, but it was my equal, my guide, my acquaintances who we took counsel together and walked unto the house of God in company, their thoughts and prayer is when will he die and his name perish, when will he fall into mistakes and error, when will their marriage hit the rock, when will his company collapse? But these are their own thoughts and not that of God. Jeremiah 29 v 11. Listen to me, Balaam's attempt to curse Israel did not prosper (Numbers 22 v 8) neither did the satanic fasting and prayers of those 40 evil men against Paul (Acts 23 v 12-21) therefore their negative prayers will not prevail over you and your family members in Jesus name. I pray for you that as you say the following prayers, the Lord will give you victory over negative prayers in the name of Jesus.

PRAYERS

1. O Lord, I thank your because it is your plan and thought that will come to pass in my life not that of my enemies in Jesus name.

2. Every negative prayer assigned to frustrate me and my destiny backfire in Jesus name.

3. Every negative prayer assigned to make me fall into mistakes and errors, be cancelled in Jesus name.

4. Imaginations and thoughts of the evil ones concerning me and my family, be aborted in Jesus name.

5. Any satanic priest (Balaam) hired to curse me, my work, my destiny and family, die on your assignment in Jesus name.

6. All demons backing up negative prayers for manifestation, be bound and cast out in Jesus name.

7. Every negative prayer that have ever been said against me, be wiped off by the blood of Jesus.

8. Negative prayers programmed into the sun, moon and star to affect my life, family and work backfire in Jesus name.

9. My life and destiny, that of my children and my work will not answer to the negative prayers of the enemies in Jesus name.

10. I shall testify in Jesus name.

JAN. 13: I REJECT WITCHCRAFT MANIPULATION

I REJECT WITCHCRAFT MANIPULATION IN JESUS NAME SCRIPTURES Psalm 27 v 1 – 2; Isaiah 49 v 24 – 26; Nahum 3 v 1 – 4; Micah 3 v 2 – 4; Ezekiel 21 v 21; Ezekiel 13 v 18 – 23; Galatian 5 v 19 – 20; Isaiah 42 v 13; Nahum 3 v 4 – 5; Ezekiel 8 v 7; Micah 5 v 12; Jeremiah 10 v 10 – 17; Isaiah 31 v 5; Isaiah 42 v 13; Isaiah 50 v 7 - 9

EXHORTATION

The power of witchcraft is the power of satan, who specialises in perpetrating evil. It is a major preoccupation of the devil to steal, kill and destroy. (John 10 v 10) Witchcraft is one of the wicked weapons which the devil has continued to use to destroy lives. In 1 Peter 5 v 8 – 9, the Bible tells us that the devil is a restless fellow; he goes about seeking whom he may devour. His goal is to destroy good things in every department of your life but with God on your side, he will not be able to perform his evil enterprise in your life in Jesus name. This same devil is the architect and the mastermind of manipulations.

Many destinies and promises of God in people's lives are being manipulated out of manifestation through witchcraft. In the account or parable of tares among the wheat in Matt 13 v 24 – 25; It can be seen clearly how the devil attempted to manipulate the good seeds of wheat by planting tares amongst them. Many people are experiencing failure at the edge of success, because of satanic manipulations through witchcraft. The subject of witchcraft is as old as creation. Many believers do not take it serious maybe due to inadequate knowledge of the scriptures on the subject or outright ignorance. It is a major tool in the hand of the devil to fulfil his objective. John 10 v 10. Though the witches operate an intelligent network, they gather strength through evil unity, receive attention from the devil and have representatives globally. But the Bible says in Isaiah 8 v 9 – 10 (paraphrase) an evil unholy gang-up, association, and counsel against us will turn to nothing and shall not stand. There is hope however for those who are ready to enter into the room of spiritual warfare to cancel every witchcraft manipulation. As you exercise faith and Holy anger, and pray these prayers, the Lord my God in whom I trust will intervene and deliver you from every witchcraft manipulation in Jesus name.

PRAYERS

1. My life, my destiny, reject witchcraft attack in Jesus name.

2. Every attack on my destiny sponsored by household witchcraft power, die in the name of Jesus.

3. Witchcraft agent cursing me day and night, die in the name of Jesus.

4. Every witchcraft power in charge of my case, die by fire in Jesus name.

5. Every witchcraft weapon of manipulation fashioned against me, you will not prosper in Jesus name (Isa. 54:17).

6. Every door opened to witchcraft to manipulate my destiny, be closed by the Blood of Jesus in Jesus name.

7. Every witchcraft agent assigned to monitor me in the dream, I bind you and your operations in Jesus name.

8. Altar of witchcraft raised to manipulate me, catch fire in Jesus name.

9. Witchcraft mirror positioned to manipulate my life, break and scatter in Jesus name.

10. Witchcraft networks to manipulate my breakthrough, scatter in Jesus name.

WEEK 3 JAN. 14TH

1.Now thank our God. With heart and hands and voices Who wondrous things has done In whom this world rejoices Who from our mothers' arms Hath bless'd us on our way With countless gifts of love And still is ours today.

2.Oh may this bounteous God Through all our life be near us With ever joyful heats And blessed peace to cheer us And keep us in His grace And guide us when perplex'd And free us from all ills In this world and the next.

3.All praise and thanks to God The Father now be given The Son and Holy Ghost Supreme in highest Heaven. The one eternal God Whom, earth and heav'n adore For thus it was, is now And shall be evermore.

WEEKLY CONFESSION SCRIPTURE:

Mathew 18 v 18 - "Verily I say unto you, whatsoever ye shall bind on earth shall be bound in heaven: and whatsoever ye shall loose on earth shall be loosed in heaven"

1. I reject defeat, shame and weeping this year in Jesus name.

2. I reject Had I known this year in Jesus name.

3. I reject Satanic attacks this year in Jesus name.

4. I reject contrary wind this year in Jesus name.

5. I reject mistakes & Errors this year in Jesus name.

6. I reject Accident, Sudden death and calamities in Jesus name.

7. I reject Hardship, Delay and Frustration this year in Jesus name.

JAN. 15: GOD'S PROMISES SHALL COME TO PASS

GOD'S PROMISES SHALL COME TO PASS IN MY LIFE IN JESUS NAME SCRIPTURES Ezekiel 36 v 11; Proverbs 23 v 18; Habakuk 2 v 2 – 3; Psalm 32 v 8; Numbers 23 v 19; Romans 11 v 29; Hebrew 13 v 8; Psalm 33 v 9

EXHORTATION

According to Ezekiel 24 v 14 -"I the Lord have spoken it, it shall come to pass, and I will do it, I will not go back, neither will I spare, neither will I repent, according to thy ways, and according to thy doings, shall they judge thee, saith the Lord God" God said, what He has promised you will come to pass. This is not the mind of your pastor, but of your God, your moulder, your creator, your builder, your architect, the creator of the heavens and the earth. Our God is good and ever faithful. His word is Yea and Amen. Anything He says, He does, just believe. Four key truths in that passage - God has spoken it - It shall come to pass - He will do it - He will not go back Men may change their minds, men may break their promises, men may lie, disappoint and deny you, but God will not.

Men can shift ground, men can suddenly change, men can find faults in and with you, men can take exception, men can dodge you, men can ignore you, men can be tired of you but God will not. This message is coming to you now so that you can run with it. Many have lost faith, saying this is another year again I don't know whether God will do it for me. Listen and hear, the Lord is saying if it remains one second, He will do it and so shall it be for you in Jesus name. As we embark on the following prayers all His promises will come to pass in your life in Jesus name.

PRAYERS

1. Every gang-up and evil network against God's promises in my life, work and family scatter in Jesus name.

2. God's promises for my life, work and family, begin to manifest in Jesus name.

3. O Lord, honour your promises for my life, work and family in the name of Jesus.

4. Anything in my foundation attacking God's promises for my life, work and family, host of heaven attack them in Jesus name.

5. Every evil preparation against me, my work and family in order to hinder God's promises for our lives scatter in Jesus name.

6. Yoke of stagnation, hindering God's promises in my life be scattered by fire in Jesus name.

7. By the power of the Almighty God, all my pending and hanging manifestation, be released in Jesus name.

8. Divine arrangement to facilitate my speedy results, manifest in the name of Jesus.

9. Every wicked altar waging war against God's promises for my life, scatter by thunder in Jesus name.

10. Every blessing allocated for me this year in the name of Jesus, manifest in Jesus name.

JAN. 16: CONNECT ME WITH MY DESTINY HELPERS

O LORD, CONNECT ME WITH MY DESTINY HELPERS IN JESUS NAME. SCRIPTURES Psalm 121, Psalm 123, II Corinthians 1 v 24; Exodus 14 v 24 – 31; Ruth 2, 3, and 4, Revelation 12 v 15 – 16; Psalm 116 v 5 – 7

EXHORTATION Beloved, no one can run the race of life in isolation. You cannot be a lone ranger and fulfil your purpose of creation on the earth, we need each to live life to the fullest. The agenda of God for us at redemption is a life of breakthrough, fruitfulness, abundance and help, but for all these to come to pass there are ordained seasons, divine helpers and helps that we must connect with. God is the ultimate source of help but He uses men as the means by which He sends the help our way. Life is about God linking you up with your divine helpers who will help you and not demand for anything in return. It is my prayer that the Lord will connect you with your destiny helpers this New Year in Jesus name.

PRAYERS

1. O Lord my father, I thank you for you are my source of help in Jesus name.

2. Every veil of darkness covering my divine helper from locating me burn by fire in Jesus name.

3. My divine helpers favour me by fire in Jesus name.

4. Every negative statement resisting my help, blood of Jesus, cancel them in Jesus name.

5. Every yoke of promise and fail in my life, break in Jesus name.

6. Blood of Jesus, link me up with my destiny helpers in Jesus name.

7. My divine helpers, dream of me by fire in Jesus name.

8. Help of God and Dew of help, locate me and rest upon me in Jesus name.

9. Goodness and mercy, locate my destiny helpers in Jesus name.

10. I will enjoy continuous help of God for ever in Jesus name.

JAN. 17: SHOW ME DIVINE BREAKTHROUGH DREAMS

O LORD SHOW ME DIVINE BREAKTHROUGH DREAMS IN JESUS NAME SCRIPTURES Mathew 13 v 25; Numbers 12 v 6; Gen. 28 v 10 – 16; 37 v 4 – 11; Acts 2 v 16 – 17; Job 33 v 14 – 16; Job 33 v 14 – 16

EXHORTATION

Dreams are spiritual media through which we receive information about happenings in the spirit realm. God almighty created this medium in order to pass information to us His children. Every beneficial invention that mankind has ever come up with, is mostly received through the dream channel, but just like every good thing God created, satan has perfected the art of polluting human destinies by planting evil seeds in people's lives through the medium of dreams.

• Joseph's destiny was revealed to him through dreams. Gen. 37 v 4 – 11

• Jacob's life transforming idea came through dream – Gen. 31 v 10 - 13

• Jesus Christ destiny was preserved and released for fulfilment through dream. Matthew 2 v 13; 19 – 23

• Solomon received his wisdom through dream - 1 Kings 3 v 5 – 15 I pray that the Lord will show you divine breakthrough dreams in Jesus name.

PRAYERS

1. O Lord my father, show me the secrets of my life in Jesus name.

2. My father, according to your word in Jeremiah 33 v 3, show me the secrets behind every trouble in my life in Jesus name.

3. Dreams that will change my life for the better, manifest in Jesus name.

4. Holy spirit, reveal to me my work environment, the place I am living etc. in Jesus name.

5. Every operation of demotion in my dream, die in Jesus name.

6. Powers from the pit of hell, summoning my name before any dark mirror, die in Jesus name.

7. My "Joseph" dreams, hear the word of the Lord, manifest in Jesus name.

8. Anointing for victory in my dreams, fall on me in Jesus name.

9. O Lord, show me what I need to know about my future/ tomorrow in Jesus name.

10. Breakthrough provoking dreams, manifest in my life in Jesus name.

JAN. 18: MY DRY BONES SHALL RISE AGAIN

MY DRY BONES SHALL RISE AGAIN IN JESUS NAME SCRIPTURES Rev. 11 v 11 & 12; Jeremiah 15 v 16; Hosea 6 v 1 – 3; Psalm 65 v 9 & 10; Ezekiel 2 v 2; Isaiah 63 v 9; Psalm 63 v 1 & 2; Isaiah 26 v 2 & 3; Psalm 102 v 13; Colossians 2 v 14 – 15; Mark 4 v 38 – 39; Luke 3 v 6; Titus 2 v 11; Ezekiel 37 v 1 – 12; Psalm 109 v 26 – 27 Job 42 v 10- 13;Ezekiel 12 v 25;Isaiah 61 v 7;2 Cor. 1 v 20;2 Corinthians 4 v 8 & 9;Rom 8 v 28 & 29; Ps 30 v 5&9

EXHORTATION

Psalm 68 v 1 – 2 says our God will arise and His enemies shall scatter. Who should God arise for? God is interested in fighting your battles, your enemies and making areas of "dry bones" in your life, family, home and work come alive again. Anything that brings discomfort, pain or hinders your blessings is your enemy. What you need do is to arise and call on God to scatter your enemies and make your dry bones come alive in Jesus name.

It is my prayer that all hindrances and obstacles to your blessings shall be scattered in Jesus name. Our God is a consuming fire, that can destroy your enemies by fire, so do not hesitate to call on Him. As you call on God in prayers and apply the weapons of God, all dry bones situation in your life shall be revived and resurrected, and the life of God will come upon you in Jesus name.

PRAYERS

1. O Lord arise, let dry bones situation in my life come alive in Jesus name.

2. Enemies of my destiny, introducing dry bone battles into my life, catch fire in Jesus name.

3. My father, by your sure mercies, restore me back to your original plan for my life in Jesus name.

4. Every hindrance to my glory advancement, I command in Jesus name, be pulled down.

5. All assets stolen from my destiny, I command, be restored back in Jesus name.

6. My progress under any yoke, blood of Jesus, release them in Jesus name.

7. My hopeless situation/cases, by the mercy of God, turn around for good in Jesus name.

8. Breath of the almighty, come upon all dry areas of my life in Jesus name.

9. According to Joel 2 v 25 – Anointing, Grace of God to recover my loses, envelop me now in Jesus name.

10. Every dry bone situation in my work, be turned around by fire in Jesus name.

JAN. 19: MY EXPECTATIONS SHALL BE FULL

MY EXPECTATIONS SHALL BE FULL IN JESUS NAME Ps. 38:22, Matt. 17:24, Gen. 5:1, Eccl. 11:3, Isa. 25:7, Col. 2:14 – 15, Prov. 13:12, Ps. 62:1 – 2, Prov. 23:18, Job 20:15, Isa. 49:17, Nah. 2:2, Jer. 30:19 Job 20 v 15; Psalm 38 v 22; Proverbs 13 v 12; Nahum 2 v 2; Psalm 65 v 9 – 10

EXHORTATION

Beloved, God has kept you for a while in that situation in order to build you up to be able to handle and sustain the testimonies. And now the same God is saying out of what you are passing through shall proceed thanksgiving because your expectations shall be full. The end of your expectation is thanksgiving. Many glorious expectations have been sold or being traded away in the market of the wickedness.

People's expectation are being covered, padlocked, delayed, caged, attacked, transferred, hijacked, emptied, cut off, swallowed and destroyed through satanic devices. But I have good news for you today according to Haggai 2 v 5 – 6 the Lord will arise for the fulfilment of your expectations in Jesus name. Don't give up.

He is mindful of you. He makes all things beautiful in His own time. And when He has His time with you, all things in your life will become beautiful. Every disappointment hovering over your life is hereby nullified in Jesus name. I see God turning your expectations into fulfilment as you pray these prayers in Jesus name. I see you at the top.

PRAYER

1. My expectation shall not be cut off in Jesus name.

2. My expectation shall not be caged in Jesus name.

3. My expectation shall not be diverted, hindered, monitored, attacked, manipulated, delayed in Jesus name.

4. My expectation, reject attacks in Jesus name.

5. My expectation, reject hindrances in Jesus name.

6. Monitoring agents assigned to monitor my expectation, be destroyed in Jesus name.

7. This is my season of Manifestation in Jesus name.

8. My expectation, reject destroyers and wasters in Jesus name.

9. God's promises and expectation for my life shall come to pass in Jesus name.

10. I enter into my season of expectation fulfilment in Jesus name.

JAN. 20: EVIL ATTEMPTS AGAINST MY LIFE BE ABORTED

EVIL ATTEMPTS AGAINST MY LIFE BE ABORTED IN JESUS NAME SCRIPTURES Isaiah 54 v 15; Gen. 37 v 18 – 28; Numbers 22 v 1 – 7; 1 Sam. 19 v 1 – 2; Psalm 31 v 13; John 11 v 45 – 53

EXHORTATION

Beloved, I want you to know that what you don't want you don't watch and what you don't resist has the right to remain. The enemy is making every attempt to steal, destroy and kill you, John 10 v 10. But it is you that will stop them through the power of the word and prayers before they stop you through their evil meetings or attacks. I prophecy, every evil attempt of the enemies against your life shall fail in the name of Jesus.

As a child of God you must be spiritually alert every day. Remember, that Potiphar's wife made every attempt to destroy Joseph, because he refused to enter into the act of sin with her. He was spiritually alert and that was why he could resist her tempting offer. The moment you are enjoying sin, any attack of the wicked will prevail. The Bible says, he that committed sin is of the devil - 1 John 3 v 8. As you shut the door against sin this year, the Lord will shield you and deliver you from every evil attempt against your life in the name of Jesus.

PRAYERS

1. Blood of Jesus, cover my life and family in the name of Jesus.

2. Every evil attempt to terminate my life and family this year, be aborted in the name of Jesus.

3. Evil attempt to enslave my glory this year or in future by any dark agent, be aborted in the name of Jesus.

4. Any attempt to fire arrows of mistake and error into my life, work, family or marriage, be destroyed by fire in Jesus name.

5. Every evil attempt to stop my progress, now or in future, fail woefully in Jesus name.

6. My life, rebel against evil attempts in the mighty name of Jesus.

7. All evil attempts to sabotage every good thing in my work throughout my life time, be aborted in Jesus name.

8. All evil attempts to pollute me through sex or food in my dream, in the name of Jesus, be aborted in fire.

9. Every evil attempt to paralyse me, spiritually or physically will not prosper in Jesus name.

10. Holy Ghost fire, scatter every destructive attempt made against me and my family, by anybody or power in Jesus name.

JAN. 21: I REJECT FAILURE AT THE EDGE OF SUCCESS

I REJECT FAILURE AT THE EDGE OF SUCCESS IN JESUS NAME SCRIPTURES Numbers 20:7 – 12, 23 – 28; Numbers 27:12 – 14; Deuteronomy 3:23 – 29 Acts 26:24 – 28; 2 Chronicles 26:1 – end; 2 Kings 7:1 – 17 (Note v. 17), 2 Kings 5:20 – 27;

EXHORTATION

Beloved, everyone living on the surface of this earth whether male or female has one thing or the other they want to succeed on, in terms of career, ministry, finance, marriage and life generally. Success is achieving your aim or your set goal. Nevertheless, there are hindrances and obstacles that want to stop us from realizing these aims and goals; there are failure programmers and failure activators on our ways who will never want us to achieve that which we purpose and God's plans for us. It is not the will of God for any of His children to experience any form of failure at the edge of success.

What contained in the Calvary package is a complete success which was obtained for us through the death of Jesus Christ on the cross and His resurrection. Because of this, we are to experience success in all ramifications of life. God has destined every believer for all-round success. Success is our inheritance, our redemptive right in redemption and privilege (Genesis 1:28), Acts 17:28a, says;

"For in Him we live, and move, and have our being" and Romans 14:8 says; "For whether we live, we live unto the Lord, and whether we die, we die unto the Lord; whether we live therefore, or die, we are the Lord's". These scriptures point to one crucial fact; that God owns in totality. And if He is never a God of failure, therefore we must not fail at the edge of success.

May we not fail at the terminal end of our race spiritually, financially, maritally in Jesus name (Amen). I enjoin you to pray these prayers very well and take stock of your life's events or patterns. The world is ready to celebrate an achiever and not a failure: Romans 8:19: "For the earnest expectation of the creature waiteth for the manifestation of the sons of God." You will succeed in Jesus name.

PRAYERS

1. O Lord, deliver me from failure at the edge of success, in Jesus name.

2. Organised battles against my breakthroughs at the edge of success, scatter by fire in Jesus name.

3. My breakthroughs, reject manipulation at the edge of success in Jesus name.

4. Every root of witchcraft in my family, die by fire in Jesus name.

5. Every meeting summoned to make me fail at the edge of success, scatter by fire in Jesus Name (Isaiah 8:9 – 10)

6. Altar of failure at the edge of success fashioned against my life, scatter by fire in Jesus name.

7. Satanic mandates and judgments against me at the edge of success be nullified in Jesus name.

8. Arrows of downfall at the edge of success fashioned against me, backfire in Jesus name.

9. Programmes in the heavenlies against my success, be aborted in Jesus name.

10. Bitter writings (John 13:26) in the heavenlies against my success, be nullified in Jesus name.

CONFESSION FOR GREATER ACHIEVEMENT

CONFESSION FOR GREATER ACHIEVEMENT IN JESUS NAME SCRIPTURES Beloved, when you got born again, you were born to win and God's plan for you is perpetual victory. 2 Cor. 2 v 14 in Apostle Paul's word, the moment you get born again, you are a perfume of Christ knowledge in every place.

Friend you are having victory for greater achievement, because you are appropriating the victory that is yours in Christ Jesus. Greater achievement is explicitly chronicled in Psalm 113 v 7 – 8. It is an achievement that does not answer nor is dependent on anything or anyone, does not respect scarcity, not subjected to the whim and caprices of the storms of life.

Greater achievement is one that makes for domination, it empowers you to take your rightful position in the scheme of things and enables the carrier to walk upon his or her high places. Habbakuk 3 v 19. This shall be your portion this year in Jesus name. As you pray the following prayers, you shall manifest greater achievement through this year and beyond in Jesus name. Jesus is Lord!

PRAYERS

1.   My ordained great achievement manifest in Jesus name.
2.   Pray for your pastor and his or her family.
3.   Pray for your church.
4.   Pray for one of Every Nation's
5.   Ask for the Holy Spirit's transformation in the area of resistance you targeted yesterday.
6.   My great achievement in any captivity, rebel, jump out and locate me in Jesus name.
7.   This is my year of_____,
I shall see my life grow in all around favor and over flow; I shall achieve and manifest greatness throughout this year in Jesus name.

Books by the Author

Dr. Sheka Mansaray

1. The Tears of My Father: (My Gift to the World)
2. DESERT ROSE: (WORDS FOR THOUGHTS)
3. Warfare Time: (Spiritual Warfare)
4. Carrier of Christ's Light: Arise, shine, for your light has come
5. Revelation Today (Living A life of Faith Daily Vol-1)
6. Unveiling Prosperity (INSIGHT OF PROSPERITY Vol 1)
7. Unveiling Prosperity (Curse & Blessing Vol 2)
8. Unveiling Prosperity (SPIRIT OF POVERTY Vol 3)
9. Revelation Today: (New oil daily Vol 2)
10. Pay yourself (steps to wealth)
11. Blessings of Wealth (Resource Creates Resource)
12. The Holy Spirit - My Helper-
13. Prayer Ammunitions
14. Face of Prayer

Meet the Author

Dr. Sheka Mansaray is the founder and Presiding Bishop of "Faith Embassy International Ministries (Revelation Church)" a multi- cultural, non-denominational church in Maryland USA.

Dr. Mansaray is the founder of Dr. Sheka Mansaray Ministries International, a partnership-based outreach ministry with a solid Apostolic and Prophetic Mandate.

Dr. Sheka Mansaray is also the founder of "Alpha Business Network" a network of current and future business owners. He is also The founder Presiding Bishop of Bishop's & Apostles International network a platform that raising up leaders in the body of Christ to rebuild the walls that is broken in the church. Dr. Mansaray is a gifted Poet, Writer, Philanthropist, Entrepreneur, and Author.

Dr. Sheka Mansaray is a husband, happily married to his Beautiful wife, Nanah Mansaray; and a father to their three children, daughter, Faith Mansaray; and Son, Sheka Jeremiah Mansaray Jr. and son, Joseph Ezekiel Mansaray.

SALVATION PRAYER

Give your life to the Lord.

Dear Friend, if you just prayed this prayer, I would like to welcome you into the family of God! Your sins are forgiven!

Father, I come to you in the precious name of your Son, Jesus. You said in Your Word that if I confess with my mouth that Jesus Christ is my Lord and my Savior and I believe in my heart that God has raised Him from the dead, I will be saved. I make the decision today to surrender every area of my life to the lordship of Jesus.

Jesus, come into my heart. Take out the stony heart and put in a heart of flesh. I turn my back on the world and on sin. I repent and I put my trust in You. I acknowledge that I am a sinner. I would like to thank You for dying on the cross for my sin and shedding Your blood for me so that I might be forgiven of my sin. Thank You that You rose from the dead and that one day, You are coming back for me. I confess that Jesus Christ has come in the flesh and that He is my personal Lord and Savior. Thank you, Lord Jesus, for saving me. I accept by faith the free gift of salvation. Amen (so be it).

Dear Friend, if you just prayed this prayer, I would like to welcome you into the family of God! Your sins are forgiven! This is the good news of the gospel of the Lord

Jesus Christ. You are now a child of God and you will live with Him forever. I encourage you to do several things to get to know Him. Read your Bible and pray everyday (talk to Jesus about everything in your life). Find a Bible-believing church that believes in the lordship of Jesus Christ. Be around strong believers who will encourage you and lift you up in your walk with God. Tell someone about your new-found faith and joy that only Jesus can bring.

Here is an effective way of sharing Jesus with others. Simply read it to your friends, family, and others and watch what the Lord will do.

www.ingramcontent.com/pod-product-compliance
Lightning Source LLC
Chambersburg PA
CBHW051430090426
42737CB00014B/2898